JEFFREY
BILHUBER'S
DESIGN BASICS

To life and its simple beauties

JEFFREY
BILHUBER'S
DESIGN BASICS

EXPERT SOLUTIONS FOR DESIGNING THE HOUSE OF YOUR DREAMS
BY JEFFREY BILHUBER WITH ANNETTE TAPERT
FOREWORD BY ANNA WINTOUR

RIZZOLI
NEW YORK

FIRST PUBLISHED IN THE UNITED STATES OF AMERICA IN 2003
BY RIZZOLI INTERNATIONAL PUBLICATIONS, INC.
300 PARK AVENUE SOUTH
NEW YORK, NY 10010
WWW.RIZZOLIUSA.COM

© 2003 BY JEFFREY BILHUBER

PRODUCED BY OPTO DESIGN, INC.
214 SULLIVAN STREET, 6C, NEW YORK, NY 10012

DESIGN: JOHN KLOTNIA AND
ANNE MACWILLIAMS, OPTO DESIGN

2003 2004 2005 2006 2007/ 10 9 8 7 6 5 4 3 2

PRINTED IN THE UNITED STATES OF AMERICA

ISBN: 0847825647

LIBRARY OF CONGRESS CATALOG CONTROL NUMBER: 2003 104768

IMAGES ON PAGES 3, 26, 39, 53, 59, 68-9, 71, 88, 93, 113, 131,139, 150, 160, 186,
197 © JEFFREY BILHUBER

PHOTOS AND IMAGES ON PAGES 102-3, 122-123, 124, 171 © BILHUBER INC.

DRAWING ON PAGE 176 BY JOHN LOWE © BILHUBER INC.

PHOTOS ON BACK COVER AND PAGES 4, 24, 42, 64, 101, 132-3, 144-5, 164-5, 178, 208
© FRANCOIS DISCHINGER

PHOTOS ON FRONT COVER AND PAGES 47, 56, 60, 97, 72-3, 108, 141, 168-9, 172, 183,
192 © OBERTO GILI

PHOTOS ON PAGES 2, 34-5 © KARI HAAVISTO

PHOTOS ON PAGES 13, 36, 38, 50, 76, 86, 112, 142 © FRANCOIS HALARD

PHOTOS ON PAGES 23, 62-3, 121 © THIBAULT JEANSON

PHOTOS ON PAGES 20, 44-5, 94, 96, 104, 130, 138, 157 © SCOTT FRANCES

PHOTOS ON PAGES 30-1, 67, 116-7, 127, 166, 190-1, 196 © LIZZIE HIMMEL

PHOTOS ON PAGES 6-7, 8, 14-5, 16, 32, 48-9, 54-5, 81, 84-5, 89,
92, 106-7, 134, 149, 158, 163, 175, 182, 184, 188, 194-5 © PETER MARGONELLI

PHOTO ON PAGES 152-3 © DEAN PENNA

PHOTO ON PAGES 82, 98-9, 111, 146, 187, 200 © WILLIAM WALDRON

PHOTOS ON PAGES 19, 40-1, 114-5, 199 © ANTOINE BOOTZ

CONTENTS

Jeffrey Bilhuber and I go back a long way. As the editor of *House & Garden* magazine in the late 1980s (which I boldly re-named *HG* to the dismay of the interior design community!), I knew that Jeffrey was a young designer to watch, someone with a strong, individual point of view. During this time, John Duka wrote one of his celebratedly acerbic back page Diary profiles on Jeffrey ("Prince of Stuff") hailing the designer "tall and mannered as a young Halston," and as "an American Modernist in the tradition of Billy Baldwin and Albert Hadley." However, I really first got to know Jeffrey when he worked on the design of an "Images of Haute Couture" exhibition that we produced to complement "Haute Couture," an exhibit at the Costume Institute of the Metropolitan Museum of Art in 1996.

This involved making coherent visual sense of a vast collection of treasures from the Condé Nast archives and elsewhere, the inspiring work of artists and photographers that documented a century of high fashion. Jeffrey placed these images in striking formations over textured plasterwork panels that lined the hallway of the Egyptian gallery for the night of the gala that inaugurated the show and which were later easily transferred to Larry Gagosian's gallery uptown: a stylish and practical solution to the constraints involved in the project.

Seeing Jeffrey at work, deftly and tactfully juggling all the different challenges and personalities involved, I realized that he was someone I could work with on my own projects, someone who wasn't going to impose his taste.

Since then, Jeffrey and I have worked together on my homes in Manhattan and on Long Island and I have realized that he is someone who is great at taking one's own taste and making it better. He doesn't have an ego, and that is rare in this business. Whether he's dealing with my son Charlie, who spent an afternoon

9

at Argosy going through endless maps until he found some very rare document from Hannibal's travels, or working with my daughter on her *Hairspray* shrine, Jeffrey took finding the perfect frames for them just as seriously as taking time and trouble with his grandest Park Avenue client; he's not a snob. And I think he's a genius when it comes to hanging pictures and he does it so fast. One. Two. Three. Amazing. It's something he's always had a special gift for; in the *Vogue* story that we produced to celebrate his work in the February 2002 issue, we photographed a wonderful house in Pennsylvania that was one of his first projects, a house that he has been refining for nearly two decades. However, one of the first things he did there was a striking dining room where he hung the clients' collection of nineteenth-century fern pictures in a wonderfully unexpected, free-flowing way around the walls. I think this room really made the design world sit up and take notice of his talent.

And of course, Jeffrey is just so much fun to be with, he's so interested in so many different things, and he's one of the wittiest people to spend time with, which of course makes the whole process so much more appealing. He can fully understand what someone is about. For instance, he is now working on the retrospective of Manolo Blahnik's work ("Manolo Blahnik, the Shoe: Celebrating 30 Years of Design") at the Phillips de Pury Luxembourg Gallery, here, he is professional and businesslike as always, but he will also make it whimsical and fun, capturing the spirit of the subject.

Clearly, Jeffrey does have his own point of view which I recognized all those years ago at *HG* and I think that came across in the *Vogue* story, but he isn't married to it. He's very open to ideas and unexpected, serendipitous inspirations. Talking of serendipity, when we were laying out that story, I wanted to incorporate an image that would evoke the magic of Nantucket, an island that Jeffrey feels a great connection with. Although he was keen for a photograph of Billy Baldwin's house there—both the man and his interiors have been great inspirations for him over the years—I chose a photograph of a pretty rose-clad cottage instead, as this said more to me about the spirit of the island. Months later, an island realtor who had seen the *Vogue* story called Jeffrey and told him that "his" house was coming on the market, and now he is firmly ensconced there!

Incidentally, I decided to put that profile feature into a *Vogue* issue celebrating American style in all things, because for me Jeffrey is dedicated to American style himself—his work is honest, practical, inventive, brisk, stylish, modern. It takes from the past but is never enslaved to it. Jeffrey is engaged by the present and the future. He is an eternal optimist.

Dear Reader, Every good decorator makes his reputation not by being a creative trail-blazer, but by making great design happen for his clients. We are paid to sweat every detail of each project, from making the big financial decisions to coming up with a game plan and narrowing the field of options. But most important, we take the fear and trepidation out of decision making so our clients can enjoy the enormous pleasures of designing and living in their homes.

One of my favorite clients came to me as a young single woman, anxious and unsure of the design process. She had never worked with a decorator before, and she had the normal worries of any decorating novice. Would she waste her money? Would she make mistakes? Would she end up turning her apartment into a mad circus of messes?

What I taught her as we worked together is that design and decorating are really a series of connected and informed choices about scale, color, fabrics, furniture placement, and decorative details. By sharing my perspective with her, she began to grow familiar and more comfortable with the tools of the design trade, its materials, and its vocabulary. Gradually, this client began to trust our approach, fell in love with the process, and became one of our firm's biggest fans. She absolutely revels in her gorgeous new home.

Now it's your turn.

Anyone can understand and use the concepts of great design. This is not a new idea. In recent years, more and more people have been paying attention to interior design, and home-furnishing retailers and do-it-yourself publications have flourished. But despite this serious flurry of interest and information, a lot of otherwise savvy people find themselves confused and discouraged in solving basic interior decoration issues. Why didn't the new paint and carpet transform your home into the polished rooms you lust for in

magazines? Is it you, or that awful man at the paint store who seemed so sure Burnt Sienna was the best color for your kitchen? Somehow, your choices and purchases don't fulfill your expectations, and you're ready to call it quits.

Don't give up. You still can have the home of your dreams. What I'm about to share with you is the accumulated wisdom of my twenty years in the business. For too long, design professionals have shrouded their craft in a veil of mystery, hoping to impart an air of prestige and exclusivity. I'm going to let you in on a secret: The truth is that good, sound design principles are simple and don't necessarily have to cost you your life savings. Whether you're hungry for a radical home makeover, sick of the cramped atmosphere of your tiny studio apartment, or just want to organize your bookshelf, this book will provide invaluable information that will help you accomplish your goals.

My intention in this book is to help you to feel confident enough to create great living spaces that complement the kind of life you and your family really live: a home where you can cook for friends, read in bed, or enjoy the perfect martini. As our lives become ever more pressured and stressful, our homes need, more than ever, to serve as havens and as affirmations that life is still sweet. Decorating is more than an investment in furniture and materials. It's an investment in living.

1 | MEETING THE DESIGNER, MEETING YOURSELF

PERSONALITY IS EXPRESSED through the juxtaposition of form and materials. Instead of framing the black and white collages over the sofa, I simply used push pins to attach them to the walls creating a room that was both glamorous and relaxed.

The most important quality a decorator has to offer is vision.

Not that a decorator has any sort of monopoly on vision, but we can certainly take what we see, combine it with our client's desires, and conjure up a picture of what the successful end result might be. In my own twenty-year career, I've discovered that most of my clients have strong ideas about how they want to live—the colors they like, the feelings and moods that seduce them, the shapes they find attractive. A decorator, however, sees beyond what's immediately known to the client. Within minutes of walking into a furnished or unfurnished space, I instinctively understand its inherent

MEETING THE DESIGNER, MEETING YOURSELF

CHAPTER ONE

advantages and weak spots and begin to formulate how best to adapt the space, and its contents, to my client's tastes and needs. A good design professional seeks to sketch a portrait of the client's life that is cohesive and coherent, wherein each choice validates the next, from room to room. As each room and its neighbors begin to take shape, an autobiographical picture slowly develops as expressed by the house and its owner.

As you delve into this book, you'll discover that interior

design is nothing more than mastering the process of expressing yourself using the experiences and materials of your own life. What you bring to the project—vision, personal belongings, memories, and dreams—is every bit as important as understanding the basic principles of decoration, which I'll be

Solutions are never found
in a single purchase.

teaching you in the following pages. To that end, this book is about understanding that a decorator's job is to discover who you are. In other words, meeting the designer is meeting yourself.

Whether you're decorating a new space or reinventing your old one, the goal is to identify what you want from your living space and what your life demands in terms of function and comfort. This requires a bit of soul searching, some inventory taking, and a realistic—yes, I said realistic—wish list of exactly what you want your living environment to be. By choosing to design your house in line with the way you live, you are establishing your own tradition—a tradition that can be passed to your children and your children's children.

Remember the advice I give all my clients: "We're not making an investment in furniture; we're making an investment in living." Money will, of course, have to be spent, but good design needn't break the bank. The first thing you must do is curb the impulse to buy. Instead, learn to spend your money wisely before you hit the stores running. A good designer will give you informed and enlightened decisions no matter what

[THESE SUMMER TOMATOES in wooden African bowls add a level of simple beauty to a kitchen.]

your budget. I promise you that there's always an appropriate and accessible solution to all of your decorating needs. Solutions are not generally found in singular purchases, but in the way those purchases mesh to create a vision and mood that wasn't there before. After all, where do you go to shop for atmosphere, or charm, or warmth, or personality, or pride? Furthermore, decorating is not necessarily an additive process. You'll be surprised to discover that the majority of your most satisfying design solutions will come as a result of removing unnecessary clutter, reconfiguring cramped or unusable rooms, or simply relocating furniture you already own. So put your cash, checks, and credit cards away for the moment, and instead reflect upon the inherent joy of learning how to identify and invite the furnishings, fabrics, textures, and colors you truly love into rooms you really need. Learning to be a designer is learning about yourself.

FROM WISH LIST TO WORK-LIST: OR HOW TO AVOID DESECRATING YOUR DECORATOR OR PUTTING OUT A CONTRACT ON YOUR CONTRACTOR

If your decoration project requires structural changes, or complex details, you may need a professional interior designer or a contractor. This is particularly true if you live in a condominium or co-op where stringent board restrictions require a licensed professional to perform even the simplest structural alterations and modifications of utility systems such as water lines and electrical circuitry.

One of the most difficult elements of the decoration and renovation process is finding a skilled decorator or contractor

THE SPACE in the background was formerly a bedroom. With the addition of a door it now acts as a library and guestroom, which in turn provides more functional public space for the family.

who understands the scope and feel of the work you want. Rather than running to the yellow pages, the best way to proceed is to ask friends or colleagues who've recently completed a renovation or redecoration. But remember, it's your responsibility to make proper inquiries and ask the right questions. Casting about for a decorator or contractor on your own is nothing more than taking the time to do a thorough investigation and then, once the candidates are lined up, listening to your instincts. Interview as many firms as you can and ask to speak to past clients and see jobs that the firm has recently completed—not just photographs, but the actual places themselves. Nothing will give you a more immediate grasp of the quality of their creativity and workmanship than standing in a space they've completed.

On another note, find out if the prospective professionals have ever sued or been sued by anyone. This can be as easy as making one surreptitious phone call or an online visit to the Better Business Bureau or county courthouse. Should you feel at all guilty or uncomfortable about this cloak-and-dagger sleuthing, just remind yourself that shelling out regular checks in the $5,000 to $25,000 range entitles you to certain rights of reference, and anyone who is unwilling to grant you as much should be avoided.

This brings me to another point in the neighborhood of nitty-gritty: insurance and bonding. These days, many apartment buildings and township planning commissions have minimum requirements for designers and contractors. Believe it or not, it's your job to find out from the city or your building's board what they are. Also check your apartment building's

THIS HOUSE sitting on a river is the ultimate sun-drenched retreat filled with self-expression.

alteration agreement, local city ordinances, or housing organizations to familiarize yourself with guidelines that determine at what times and on what days major alterations can take place. Even for freestanding homes, construction noise and dumping procedures are major concerns for you and your neighbors. Until you've gathered all such details, it will be impossible for you to come up with a valid deadline or a reasonably calculated budget.

Another issue is finding out the size of your decorator's or contractor's workforce and exactly how many projects they are currently engaged in. Do they have the time to pay full attention to your needs? Fast-forwarding to the conclusion of a project, you should never agree to pay them in full until you have gone through a thorough "punch list" of all outstanding details and ensured that everything has been taken care of to your satisfaction. This may sound like professional tug-of-war, but a reputable professional won't find this at all unsuitable and, in fact, will be pleased to see that the work has been inspected prior to signing off.

While we're on the topic of contractual obligation, don't forget to keep your side of the bargain too. Pay promptly when you're presented with invoices. Without timely payment, creativity, materials, and craftsmen may fail to materialize. Once you've hired your interior designer and contractor, don't expect them to be on the site every day—that's not their job. This is a common misconception. An efficiently operated decorative team or contractor's crew will have a project manager and a job foreman (or a series of foremen) at the project site to carry out

IN MY OWN APARTMENT, I wanted to maximize the amount of natural light, emphasize the high ceilings, and play to the therapeutic aspects of a neutral palette.

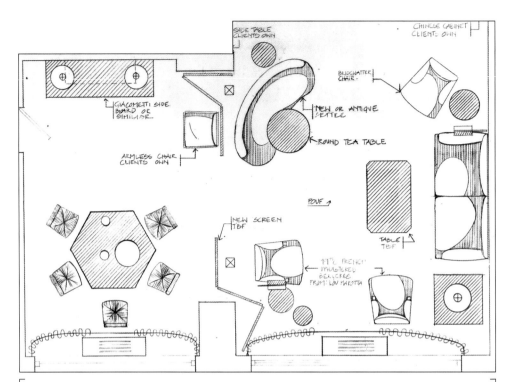

The labels on the furniture plan read:

SIDE TABLE CLIENTS OWN · CHINESE CABINET CLIENT OWN · GIACOMETTI SIDE BOARD OR SIMILIAR · BRUGNATTER CHAIR · NEW OR ANTIQUE SETTEE · ROUND TEA TABLE · ARMLESS CHAIR CLIENTS OWN · POUF · NEW SCREEN TBF · TABLE TBF · 17TH FRENCH UPHOLSTERED BERGERE FROM: LOU MAROTTA

A FURNITURE PLAN is the first lesson to understanding how your pieces will fit into your rooms and how you will move through the space (above). THE FIRST STEP in learning to read blueprints is to understand the symbols (right).

the day-to-day job management. They should be your liaison to the progress and quality-control issues on the minor and immediate level. Bigger issues, of course, are resolved with the principals, meaning your decorator and contractor.

GETTING STARTED FROM THE GROUND UP: BRING ON THE BLUES

Should you decide to move further with both a decorator and a contractor, you're surely going to need to read and understand the significance of blueprints.

The majority of my clients, being otherwise highly intelligent, are somehow mortified to admit that they're baffled when confronting those expensive little hieroglyphics that represent their homes. So if you don't know how to read blueprints, just think of them as a sort of virtual reality on paper; the visual representation of an idea through which you can stroll with a pencil and paper, asking questions and proposing changes as you go. With each new version, your house will begin to take on a life of its own; something new or different will no doubt reveal itself to you as you begin to better know and master your living space and the process by which it becomes your home.

EIGHT SYMBOLS YOU CAN'T DESIGN WITHOUT

⊖ Duplex Receptacle

$ Switch

$_D Dimmer Switch

Ceiling Mounted Fixture

▽ Telephone Receptacle

▽ Fax Receptacle

ⓒ Cable TV Receptacle

ⓢ Smoke Detector

EXISTING PLAN / DEMOLITION PLAN

The very first blueprint is called an Existing Plan, which, as the name suggests, shows the present conditions of the house or apartment as is: there's that ugly kitchen, there's that partition wall that simply has to go, there's the electrical outlet and plumbing in just the wrong place. Think of the Existing Plan as a starting point, a kind of "You Are Here" place on the map when beginning the process of redirecting your house.

The next step is to create a Demolition Plan, which is similarly self-explanatory—a plan that takes into account all of the structural alterations you intend to make. (You see how easy this is....) In formatting professional plans (which sometimes combine both existing and demo information), demolition work is indicated by dotted lines and proposed construction is crosshatched.

Learning to read a blueprint or, more specifically, a floor plan, is crucial to remaining on top of your project: if you don't know what you're looking at, you can't possibly know what you're getting—or, more important, what you're paying for. Those squiggly little lines in an electrical plan are not there solely for your amusement; each one has a dollar value. Every new outlet, switch plate or sconce location added to the plan costs more money. Multiply that by building-code regulations (which require an outlet every six feet or so) and you'll quickly understand why I advocate scrutinizing your blueprints the way you do a restaurant check. This way, when you come to the inevitable problem ("Honey, I think we have to move that wall six feet to the left"), you are well aware of just what it entails in terms of time and cost. You also will be able (in certain instances) to happily inform your contractor and carefully inform your spouse that, all things considered, a six-foot extension cord will do just fine.

If you're asking yourself what all this paperwork has to do with beautiful rooms, let me assure you that while construction and decorating are generally thought to be entirely separate processes, they must be conceived in tandem. For example, how can you establish an electrical plan if you haven't given at least some thought to where your furniture will be

Great decoration takes your taste and makes it better.

placed within the room? There's nothing more irritating than sitting down to read in the living room and having to turn on the lights in the kitchen to do it! In this example, as in so many instances, nothing more than poor planning is to blame. So just say no to obstacle courses in your home: merely by keeping your ideal use of the space (that is, how you plan to live in it) in mind from the very earliest stages, you'll rest assured that each room will give back maximum comfort and benefits for every dollar you've spent.

29

PROPOSED PLANS / ELEVATION PLANS

A Proposed Plan shows relative placement of furniture in each room and indicates numerically which elevations (cut away views seen from eye level within the room) you will see as you move through them. Once again hieroglyphics come into play: think of the diamond-shaped symbols as a directional compass that tells you what view you are looking at as you stand in that particular spot. To "look into" any of these views, simply turn to the correspondingly numbered Elevation Plans, which will illustrate the room/view indicated.

With elevation plans you now can really begin to orient yourself within the space and start to get an idea of how such things as paintings, curtains, and wall sconces will look. This is wonderfully practical information to have early on, not only for decorative purposes but also for more functional aspects of planning your home. If you're left-handed, for example, you'll want to be sure that all the switches aren't on the right side of your doors. Think of elevations as a form of preconstruction troubleshooting, helping to identify potential problem-solving decisions and matters of preference before they become problems or oversights. If time is money in the business world, timing is money in the design world. By establishing and adhering to a careful and informed order of events, most problems can be deftly side-stepped before it's either too late, too difficult, or too expensive to correct them.

IMAGINATION can be triggered by something you find in an antique
shop or something found in nature. For this oceanside residence,
I used shells to express a sense of place.

Learning to be a designer
is learning about yourself.

THIS FAMILY ROOM is the perfect blend of the clients' personality and their needs. As in most rooms, function and comfort are paramount, but never have to compromise design.

INITIALIZING YOUR DESIGN GOALS

Here are a series of questions I ask my clients. I have discovered that they assist in the soul-searching process of realizing their decorative goals.

DO I NEED TO HAVE THE PROJECT COMPLETED BY A CERTAIN DATE?

- Family reunion
- Holidays
- Birth of a child
- Other

WHAT ARE MY DESIGN PRIORITIES?

- The living room has been without comfortable furniture for long enough.
- It's time I treated myself to a beautiful master bedroom.
- I'm tired of eating in the kitchen; I want a dining room.
- I'm bored with my current color scheme.
- My kitchens and bathrooms need a face-lift.

WHAT IS MY BUDGET BOTH SHORT-TERM AND LONG-TERM?

- What funds are immediately available?
- Will the changes I envision require financial planning?

GIVEN THIS INFORMATION, DO I WANT TO START ON A MASTER PLAN OR A PHASED PLAN?

- A master plan is a step-by-step process that takes the design comprehensively from beginning to end.
- A phased plan breaks down the master plan down into grouped priorities that are accomplished over an extended period of time.

Now that you know how to hire a contractor, and make sense of blueprints, ask yourself if you have what it takes to quarterback a design project. Given what you've learned here and what you will learn in the following chapters, you might well discover that you can be your own decorator. My goal is to give you the power to use your creativity in an enlightened and organized way. ■

2 | TUNING IN

THE GREATEST QUALITY of this spacious bedroom is its oversized east-facing window. I positioned the bed to face the morning sun to capitalize on this feature.

As I wrote this book, I imagined two types of readers. One was the first-time decorator. The other was someone who had already attempted to decorate his or her own home, but ended up less than satisfied with the result. If you're the former, congratulate yourself on the time and money you've saved by committing to learning about the process before you begin. Aren't you lucky? If you're the latter, you're now at the point where you understand why many people turn to professionals. You also understand why it's important to develop your skills so that your next stab

TUNING IN
CHAPTER TWO

at decorating is a more rewarding experience. Let's start by thinking about what initially attracted you to your living space. Was it the view? Or the scale of the rooms? Maybe it was the fireplace in the bedroom, or the way the light comes through the windows in the morning. Walk through your rooms and ask yourself what their best qualities are. If you listen to your immediate responses, you'll reconnect with the essence of what first seduced you and realize that those features are still there, ready to be enhanced.

WHEN I SKETCHED this dining room for a client it reconfirmed the qualities that I first noticed in the room. High ceilings allowed me to introduce a pair of tall doors and a large window was emphasized to accentuate the view (above). A DETAIL OF THE ROOM featured on page 36 shows that even in a large space, pockets of intimacy are possible (left).

BENJAMIN MOORE, HARBOR FOG, 2062-70

OFTEN YOUR ROOM'S best feature will go unnoticed unless you confront it with a direct opposite. For this barn, I played up its rustic qualities by lacquering the floor in white enamel.

Rethink your ideas
of what a room should be.

Now that you have a list of your home's good points, the next step is to make a realistic, function-specific list of every-thing you hope to get out of your envi-ronment. So pick up a pencil and paper and spend a few minutes carefully con-sidering your living space in relation to your current lifestyle, domestic habits, and even your future aspirations. For exam-ple, many of my younger clients don't feel they need a dining

Nothing you really like is ever out of style.

room and as a result their kitchens or family rooms are becom-ing much more important. While certain rooms may currently serve multiple functions, it is a good idea to start out with a specific wish list of must-haves and ideal situations for each room. You can then blur the boundaries of what the room can do or should be.

If more than one person is making decisions or sharing the space, copy the following questions and work separately so that each person's ideal vision is brought to light. When you review and share your responses, you may be surprised to learn just how many roles your house is required to play but delighted to discover that by way of intelligent design, you can dramatically improve its performance and visual allure. Whatever you do, don't restrict yourself to just one idea; the best living spaces evolve from looking at rooms from

A NINETEENTH CENTURY Sheridan side chair provides welcome relief from the modern design of this urban kitchen.

Celebrate the way you live.

THE BIG QUESTIONS

- Do I like the proportions of the room?
- What direction does the room face?
- Does it get light in the morning or in the afternoon?

Take your bedroom, for example. If the windows face east, you probably get morning light. If waking to natural daylight pleases you, place your bed facing the window. If you like to sleep in, another solution is required. Instead of the wrought-iron bed you coveted, consider a solid upholstered or wooden headboard, which will be much more effective in blocking morning rays.

- What do I like most about the room?
- What do I like least?

The answers to these questions can be further enhanced by knowing early on that areas you like least need to be diminished, either architecturally or decoratively. Certainly, a room's most alluring qualities will dictate the furniture and decorative decisions so that these attributes are highlighted and better appreciated.

- How many functions does this room need to perform?

Increasingly, rooms have to be multifunctional. An office by day is the dining room by night. This means that wiring for telephones and computers needs to be incorporated into a room that never had those requirements. Correspondingly, a sideboard can be refitted to be the perfect storage component for office-related files as well as your china.

- Do I feel comfortable entertaining here, or are these rooms just for me?

These questions pertain to the public rooms in the house: the living room, family room, library, and dining room. Bedrooms are not considered public spaces and are therefore not part of the equation. However, just because it's a living room doesn't mean it's built for entertaining. Perhaps you and your family are content just keeping it for your own pleasure. And, if you know that for you, a dinner party means entertaining in a restaurant, then perhaps you don't need seating for twelve in the dining room; four chairs will suffice.

- Is this room going to be used for more formal purposes, or more casual family-oriented events? Do I even know what formal is anymore?
- Of the furniture that I currently own, what pieces do I like? What pieces do I hate? Is there furniture from another room that could work successfully in another part of the house?

There's invariably a moment in the design process when you will reach your financial limit. This is the moment when that ugly sofa just might turn out to be a swan in disguise. With a new slip-cover or cushion, a hard seat becomes soft or an unattractive arm becomes graceful.

- When it comes to furniture and decoration do I prefer modern or traditional shapes? Is there a remote possibility that given some enlightenment and confidence I might just (horrors!) find the courage to mix both types in one room?

Often, people will flip through design magazines and not be able to articulate what attracts them to photographs of certain rooms. Many times, it's the designer's assured ability to artfully mix different cultures, periods and styles. This mix is what introduces inherent personality to a room.

several angles. Don't be afraid to change the way you see these rooms—or use them.

Answering the big questions helps you put your decorative goals into the proper perspective. You're now on your way to the perfect marriage of knowledge and creativity. By zeroing in on what you want, you get the foundation for what you can have—both decoratively and financially. We've now paved a realistic path to deciding on the materials, colors, textures, and furniture that will successfully enact this plan.

WHEN DEFINING YOUR TASTE, don't limit yourself to a particular school of furniture. Modern and traditional can coexist with great harmony (above). THE POSITIVE IN THIS LIVING ROOM was the natural light. The negative was its compact size. By adding mirrors on either side of the fireplace we doubled the size of the room and enhanced the positive (previous spread).

3 | FEAR-FREE DECORATING:
    DID YOU HEAR BELLS AND WHISTLES?

Many times new clients will tell me they're convinced they could never decorate their own house because they don't know what they like. I always tell them that, at the very least, they probably know what they don't like. If you can figure out what you don't want, it certainly helps narrow the field in defining the décor you do want. Happily, when it comes to interior decorating, the half-empty glass is really half-full, and the empty glass overfloweth.

Trust me! Don't be terrified to make decisions. By recognizing that we all have the instinctive gift to respond to color, form, and the overall feel of any space, you have already taken the first step toward unleashing the designer within. So to those who panic at the idea of making aesthetic choices, remember this: the act of creating beauty around us is a natural, organic process that we all undertake—consciously or not—every day. In fact, you've been doing it all your life. Remember when your parents finally asked the big

FEAR-FREE DECORATING: DID YOU HEAR BELLS AND WHISTLES?

CHAPTER THREE

TO CHOOSE THIS ANIMATED console and mirror took a lot of courage on the part of my clients, and the risk paid off. An entryway is a perfect place to assert yourself.

question "What color would you like your room to be?" Was there a wave of excitement? Were you terrified? Probably not. In fact, I bet you were bursting to have a say. All of a sudden, you were in the position of making a decision about what you

We all have the instinctive gift to respond to color, form, and the overall feel of any space.

like, and I would bet that even as a child, you knew exactly what shade of blue or orange you wanted. You need to reconnect with that instinctive voice. By identifying and building on natural decision-making instincts, we can begin to envision how decorative choices can become focused and applied to the way we live.

Another way to avoid the unexpected and potentially humiliating attack of Decorating Paralysis (medically known as *Chinesemodernbaroquetradish ecoli*) is to recognize that a well-designed house is not something that happens all at once. Rather, it can (and in most cases should) be approached in small doses that build to a bigger picture. Think in medical terms. If you feel unwell, it's not the first pill that's going to work the miracle, but rather a prescribed sequence of medication over a set period of time that slowly contributes to the desired end result: good health. Likewise, a good house is the result of a series of layered relationships between its different parts.

A FLOATING BED dramatically turns its back on the entrance to the room, providing privacy and decorative flair.

FIGURING OUT YOUR BUDGET Part of fear-free decorating is figuring out the money part. Some of my clients are afraid to jump into decorating because they worry about ballooning costs. Never start a project before outlining the budget. This will help you prioritize what you'd like to get done, give you a realistic idea of how much decorating work costs, and prevent any unpleasant surprises when you get your Visa bill at the end of the month. A good decorator can help you with this process, but if you're on your own, try the outline on page 58.

You can approach your budget in two ways: start with a total and allocate it room by room, or you can do it the way I prefer, which is to analyze each room from the perimeter and work

BENJAMIN MOORE, GRANT BEIGE, HC-83

THE LIVING ROOM should be your starting point for your decorating project. The palette and textures shown here assisted in making decisions for the rest of the house.

Unleash the designer within.

your way in. This means starting with the ceiling and the walls and determining their finishes and details. Next is the floor, and you need to determine not only the finish but also the covering. As you begin to work your way into the room, window

What we don't put in a room is more important that what we do put in.

treatments logically follow. Once the shell is complete, you can work your way through the decorative program of freestanding electrical lighting, upholstery, case goods, and the final decorative accessories. This process, when followed from room to room, ensures that nothing in the budget has been forgotten.

DECIDING WHERE TO BEGIN One of the most common mistakes that people make is to first focus all their energy and resources on the most frequently used rooms. Kitchens and bathrooms are almost always the guilty party for the simple reason that people know the laundry list of items needed for these rooms. "I need a refrigerator." Check. "I need a dishwasher." Check. "And a sink. Oh, boy, we're really on a creative tear, now!" Double check! What happens is that you end up putting so much time and, I might add, money into these rooms that you're going to use up more than their fair share of the budget. You think you're making great creative strides, but before you know it,

ONCE YOU GAIN CONFIDENCE there are endless possibilities. Here, a Chinese bowl, an African stool, and a 1940s chair work together effortlessly.

HOW TO BUILD A BUDGET

USE THE FOLLOWING OUTLINE TO FIGURE OUT YOUR BUDGET. ASSIGN
THE DOLLAR VALUES YOU THINK OR KNOW YOU CAN AFFORD FOR EACH ITEM.

FINISHES *WALLS/CEILINGS/TRIM/*
DOOR/MILLWORK*

$_____ PAINT
$_____ PAPER

FLOORS *MEASURE THE SQUARE FOOTAGE*
OF EACH ROOM YOU PLAN ON DECORATING.
THIS WILL HELP YOU CALCULATE COSTS
IF YOU PURCHASE CARPETS OR RUGS.

$_____ HARDWOOD
$_____ CARPET/RUGS
$_____ TILE/STONE

WINDOW TREATMENTS *INCLUDES CURTAINS,*
SHADES, AND BLINDS

$_____ HARDWARE X # OF WINDOWS
$_____ FABRIC X # OF WINDOWS

HARDWIRED LIGHTING *REFERS TO ANY WORK*
THAT REQUIRES AN ELECTRICIAN

$_____ WALL SCONCES
$_____ PICTURE LIGHTS
$_____ PENDANT FIXTURES
$_____ CHANDELIERS

FREESTANDING ELECTRICAL
OR DECORATIVE LIGHTING

$_____ STANDING LAMPS
$_____ TABLE LAMPS
$_____ READING LIGHTS

UPHOLSTERY *THIS MEANS ANY*
SOFT FURNISHINGS.

$_____ SOFAS
$_____ CHAIRS
$_____ OTTOMANS

CASE GOODS *THIS MEANS ANY HARD*
FURNISHING YOU BUILD OR BUY MADE
OF WOOD.

$_____ SIDE TABLES
$_____ COFFEE TABLES
$_____ ARMOIRES
$_____ BENCHES

ACCESSORIES OR DECORATIVE TOUCHES

$_____ ARTWORK
$_____ VASES
$_____ CERAMICS
$_____ ANTIQUES
$_____ ANYTHING THAT HELPS
_____ FINISH THE ROOM
_____ *(CANDLES, PLANTS, ETC.)*

$_____ TOTAL

* *Millwork is any feature built into*
the wall, such as built-in bookshelves
or convector covers.

you've run out of funds and you're staring at porch furniture in your living room. That's great on *Green Acres*, not so great in Great Neck. I strongly urge you to save kitchens and bathrooms for last. These two rooms can be the most costly, and they have less impact than other rooms. Maybe a major renovation of the kitchen is not even necessary after all. Perhaps you can make a change with a coat of paint, or by replacing the hardware. Or why not just go out to dinner, for God's sake? By the time you get to the kitchen, you will understand the great joy of a decorative sleight of hand. Who knows? Porch furniture in the kitchen may not be such a bad idea.

The living room, or the not-so-living-room, as the case may be, is often the best place to start. Where better to plan your first domestic triumph than in one of the larger and more public rooms in your house? I'm talking domestic bliss, baby! Social triumph! Jealous neighbors! The works! By focusing your attention on establishing the essential tone and feel of the living room (most of them look directly into the entry or dining room), you will have established a mood that will then inform the rest of your project. Remember that good decoration should have a strategic long-term game plan but be allowed to evolve over time. Are you beginning to see the picture? You'll narrow down your personal preferences

WHAT COULD BE MORE FUN than testing your courage in a guestroom? Here, I placed two twin mattresses end to end, creating a bold corner sofa effect. Daring is further amplified by the mirrored walls.

and ensure that you never run headlong into a color that makes you scream. Soon enough, you'll become increasingly aware of the spirit, materials, proportions, and choices that best suit your personality and the way you live.

Still feeling somewhat less than fearless? Then remember this: design decisions are nothing more than opportunities. They're opportunities to express ourselves as well as opportunities to reflect and accommodate our way of life. These opportunities present themselves to us all day long. It starts

HOW TO DETERMINE AREAS OF PRIORITY:

BEFORE YOU BEGIN TO CONSIDER THE DOLLARS AND CENTS OF DECO-RATING AND RENOVATING, I INSIST THAT YOU PRIORITIZE THE ROOMS YOU WANT TO DECORATE FIRST AND THOSE THAT CAN BE PUT ON HOLD. THIS IS THE SEQUENCE I SHARE WITH MY CLIENTS.

ENTRY/FOYER
The autobiographical synopsis of what a visitor can expect throughout the house. This room clearly sets the stage for all the beauty that will follow. Why not put this at the top of your list?

LIVING ROOM
As the name implies, you live here. In an ideal world, this should be the heart and soul of the house. Not only does it provide the most room, but, more often than not, it boasts a fireplace, a view, and the most versatility. Don't let the kitchen hold this room hostage.

FAMILY ROOM
Obviously, it's where children and adults gather for pleasure. Keep it simple and carefree.

BREAKFAST ROOM
Rule of thumb—if you can't hose it down, don't buy it. This must be the most utilitari-an room of all and as such is a great place to use affordable and readily available furniture that is durable and decorative.

HALLWAYS
Don't ignore them, just because they're passageways. We pass through these spaces several times a day. What better way to give yourself pleasure than by making them beautiful? Think of this area as a gallery—perfect for art-work and photographs.

LIBRARY/DEN
Don't forget the importance of an intimate room—a quiet retreat. It's also a great place to explore bright colors and dramatic fabrics.

DINING ROOM
As the original purpose of this room fades, perhaps we can revisit its intent. Certainly, it can be more informal than it ever has been before. By no means does informal mean less attractive, but it does mean more economical.

KITCHEN
Ninety percent of this room's goal is function. If it works well, the decorating is minor. Unlike any other room in the house, a couple of beautiful baskets add as much as a sofa and a pair of chairs do to a living room.

BATHROOMS
Again, these rooms have a spe-cific function. Before you start ripping fixtures out, think again. Charming wallpaper, a couple of photos, and good lighting may be all you need.

MASTER BEDROOM
The children won't mind if their room isn't decorated right away. Splurge and treat your-self first; you deserve it.

CHILDREN'S ROOM
Like the breakfast room, this is an easy place to economize and invest in simple, store-bought furniture. Honestly, some functional pieces, a cheerful color, and a comfort-able bed work every time.

every morning as we decide what clothes to wear, and what colors, textures, and materials to gravitate to. So, if you're afraid to make decisions about a paint color, simplify the equation. What colors do you consistently reach for when getting dressed? Do you like dark tones or bright colors? Do you like textures or flat weaves? Do you like clothing that has sheen or do you prefer matte finishes? Information gained as painlessly as walking through your own wardrobe can help to define what you want your rooms to be. That said, let's get cracking.

THE POWER OF THIS LIVING ROOM is defined by strategic placement of mirrors, a monumental Chinese scroll, and a mid-twentieth century lantern.

4 | RELATIONSHIPS: THE ART OF ORGANIZING SPACE

For better or for worse, gone are the days when houses were built with each room dedicated to a single purpose. Modern living is about ensuring maximum versatility in your house regardless of its size. In chapter 2, we took stock of what your house has to offer in terms of light, scale, and architecture. The next phase is the Furniture Plan, or the "What goes where?" aspect of decorating. Like so many other areas of interior design, this process starts with function and comfort, which are more important than you may think. By designing a successful plan, you'll be able to create several interrelated environments within any room without compromising its overall sense of unity. If that sounds ambitious, keep in mind that our living spaces should reflect and accommodate our lives as we live them today.

RELATIONSHIPS: THE ART OF ORGANIZING SPACE

CHAPTER FOUR

A CHEST OF DRAWERS in this living room is practical for storage and decorative because it provides balance for a similarly scaled fireplace at the opposite end of the room.

The first step toward designing a versatile furniture plan is recognizing the characteristics and benefits of a room that can seamlessly accommodate and serve its occupants. A well-planned room greets its inhabitants with all the information they need to know about where they are and what's available to them in terms of comfort and hospitality. Just as a dining table says "Eat here" and an area of upholstered furniture tempts us to "Sit here," so does a clear pathway to a window beckon us to "Look here." Your furniture plan essentially directs traffic by suggesting uses and extending invitations to enjoy any number of comforts and vignettes within a room.

To illustrate: if you find yourself constantly being drawn to the same chair, in the same room, and turning on the same old lamp every night when you get home, whether you're alone or with friends, you've failed. What you need to do is develop a furniture plan that makes all the rooms in your house equally appealing, providing tempting choices about where to sit, sleep, eat, or entertain. In a library, for example, you should expect to find an area for reading or for taking a nap. The living room, by turn, should allow you to entertain both casually and formally, with at least two seating groups and perhaps a place for an informal meal. From the decorator's perspective, all of these domestic moments add up to a simple list of furnishings: a sofa, a couple of upholstered chairs, a small table, an open-backed chair or two, and perhaps a chaise lounge. These pieces—some of which you may already own—will give you the formula for several options in two rooms.

ARRANGEMENTS OF OBJECTS are not limited to furniture alone. These beautiful, organic forms have been carefully selected to create a harmonious tablescape.

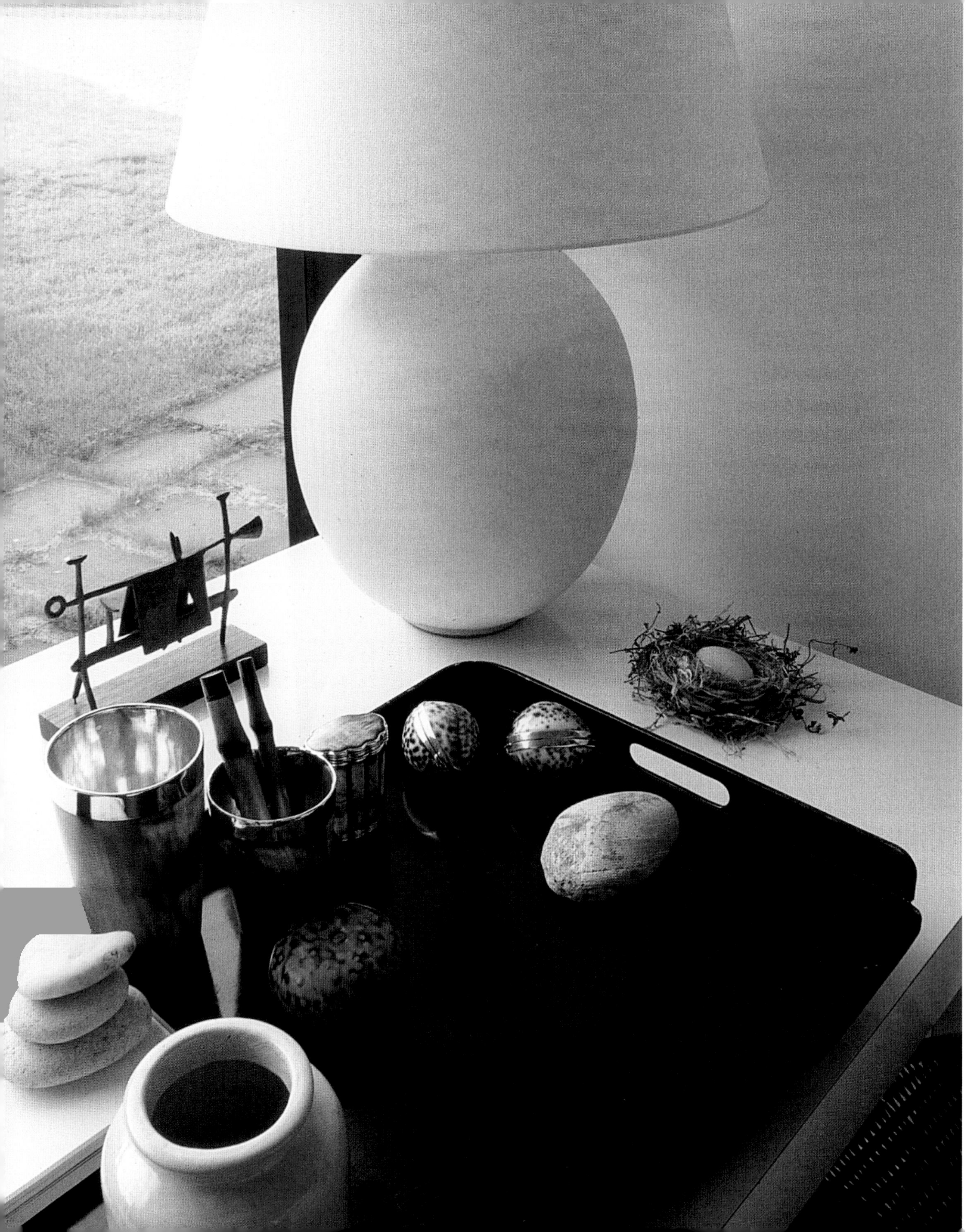

ONE FLOOR PLAN, FIVE FURNITURE PLANS

HERE WE SEE HOW ONE ROOM CAN BE TRANSFORMED BY FIVE DIFFERENT FURNITURE ARRANGEMENTS.

PLAN 1

This very light and open plan essentially uses two love seats or small sofas to create two evenly weighted furniture groupings. There is a slightly more formal approach to this resolution that would be ideal for adult entertaining like a small cocktail party, allowing neat and comfortable seating and plenty of circulation.

PLAN 2

The densest of all proposed furniture plans, the crescent-shaped sofa provides a generous and welcoming elevation as you enter the room, while the back-to-back open armchairs gently address the sofa and fireplace. The armless chair flanking the fireplace are a signature of my work, and are used to great effect as occasional chairs—note how the unexpected use of three round area rugs further the intimate qualities of this place.

PLAN 3

This plan is the most open and modern of all five. The large L-shaped or sectional sofa in the corner makes this room ideal for families with young children. Correspondingly, the pair of comfortable chairs and ottoman at the fireplace insure that this quality is not forgotten. The large area rug provides comfort with lots of child-friendly areas to play.

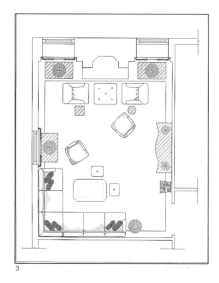

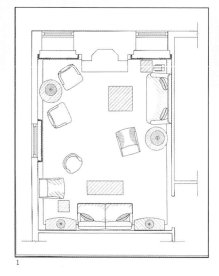

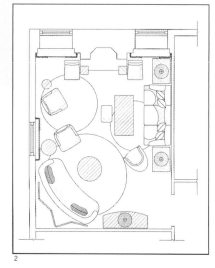

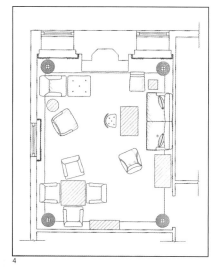

PLAN 4

This very versatile plan includes another hallmark of my work; the card or games table surrounded by dining-height upholstered chairs. This table can be used for games, lunch, or even homework. A plan like this encourages people to spend less time gathering in the kitchen and more time living in the living room. The placement of four standing lamps provides an element of symmetrical order in this otherwise asymmetrical plan.

PLAN 5

This is a classic! I developed a similar furniture plan when I first started my business twenty years ago, and I continue to use variations of it successfully to this day. Two sofas are used again, except this time, one is small and intimate and the other, near the fireplace is large and comfortable. The back-to-back open armchairs are skillfully separated by a low screen, anywhere from thirty-two to forty-eight inches high maximum. Additional seating is provided by two small ottomans in front of the cocktail table. The two groupings of furniture are substantiated by the separate area rugs, whose split perfectly aligns with the center of the window. I've saved the best for last!

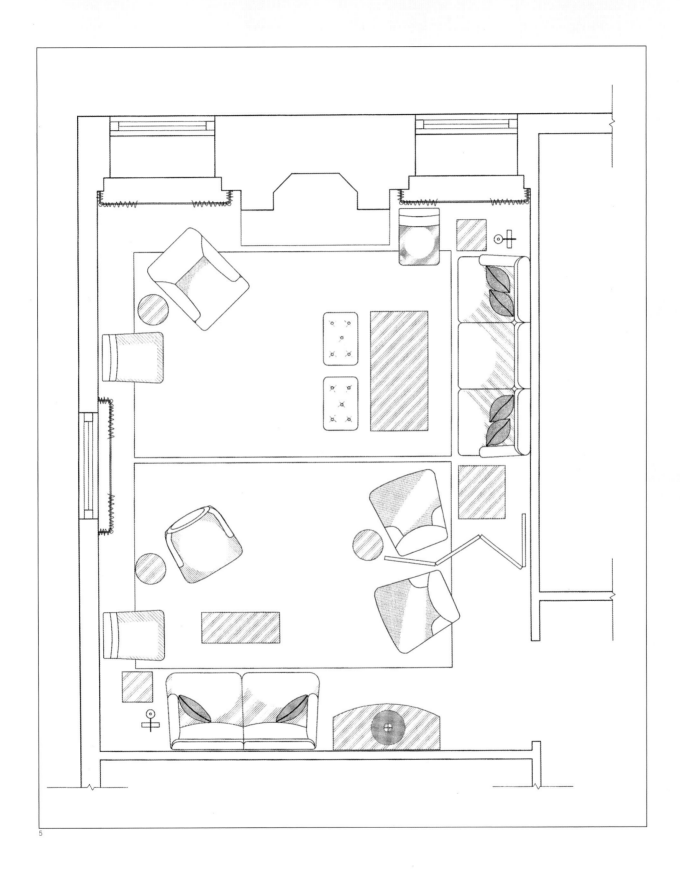

FURNITURE OPTIONS
ROOM BY ROOM

LIVING ROOM

- Start with two sofas of different sizes.
- Don't forget the importance of a card table for games or meals.
- Think asymmetrically. Don't always balance furniture so that it's centered in the room. The more original the plan, the more your personality shines through.

ENTRY/FOYER

- This space is all about the details.
- We all know a console is a necessity, but don't forget a functional mirror, a chair or bench on which to sit while removing your shoes, a basket for mail, a flattering shaded lamp, and an umbrella stand.
- Use these details to establish a visual preview of the rooms to follow.

FAMILY ROOM

- Durability drives this plan.
- The needs of modern living take precedence here. Don't forget the inclusion of the television, stereo, computer, fax machine, and book shelves. Do you want to be able to work on the computer and watch TV at the same time? If so, take this into consideration when mapping out your plan.

- It's the perfect room for an extra-large coffee table, but why not try a big upholstered ottoman with a decorative tray on top to serve the same purpose? And it will double your seating—perfect for your Super Bowl party.

BATHROOMS

- From the powder room to the master bath, don't forget the importance of a charming scaled chair or a small chest. Space permitting, the unexpected addition of furniture can turn utilitarian spaces into stylish rooms.

MASTER BEDROOM

- It's not just about the placement of the bed and chest of drawers. The addition of the following pieces turns an attractive bedroom into a luxuriously comfortable one.
- A chair and ottoman or a chaise lounge guarantees an optional place to read that doesn't involve lying in bed. Make a space for eating by adding a small round table and two small chairs.
- A dressing table liberates you from having to share a bathroom when you're trying to put on your makeup. It can also substitute as a desk when needed.
- An armoire provides more than just additional storage. It's also the perfect place to hide the television.

I could devote several long paragraphs explaining how to devise your own scaled floor plan on graph paper, but instinct tells me that you would quickly become intimidated and relegate this book to the giveaway pile. Instead, there's a fun, tangible, and yet still practical method of deciding what should go where. It's one I still do myself, and though it sounds silly, you really will learn something from it. (Warning: You may want to try this alone. Otherwise you're apt to be labeled certifiable.) What I've done, and what you should do, is put yourself in each room and imagine for a minute or two that you're a chair (yes, a chair), or a sofa, or a table, and ask yourself: "Where in this room would I want to be?" Let yourself be the chair—I'm not kidding! Ask yourself if you prefer to feel the sun on your front or back. Do you want to address the sofa on the opposite wall, or do you feel more comfortable in this location, near the fireplace? Once you've been a chair, and a very good chair you were, you can become an even better sofa. Go to the other side of the room, and figure out how the chair and sofa relate. By doing this, you're not only putting yourself in the fur-

IF POSSIBLE, WHEN ORGANIZING A FURNITURE PLAN try for at least two groupings. As in this drawing, they can be anchored by a strategic placement of area rugs.

niture's place, you're also putting yourself in the human place as well. Sit on the sofa and pretend to have a conversation with someone in the chair. Is it an easy conversation? Is there a rapport, or do you feel the need to get closer? You do? Well, then,

Imagine you're a chair: Where in the room would you want to be?

move the chair. Slowly, you're beginning to build a mythical furniture plan that will develop into a successful and realistic arrangement of furniture. (P.S. Your neighbors really were watching.)

THERE ARE NUMEROUS WAYS to bring the outdoors inside that are more creative than a potted plant by the window. The black and white canopy on the outdoor terrace is repeated indoors, which makes a strong visual connection between the two spaces.

Our living spaces
should reflect the way
we live our lives.

If you like, you can now move on to drafting a furniture plan on graph paper and drawing what you've created in your head. Or, take one of these imagined versions of your room and move it directly into the physical realm. Use stand-in pieces to see how your rooms will react to three-dimensional volume and human traffic. Old furniture can serve as placeholders: a card table and chairs as a stand-in for a dining area or workspace; a twin mattress as a sofa marker; or a cardboard box as an end table. Don't despair if a whole new houseful of furniture is not in your budget—you may not need it. You'll be surprised to find that what you already own can be slipcovered or reupholstered and simply plugged in at a new and unexpected location.

If you still think you need a scaled drawing in order to proceed, the first thing you must develop is the floor plan. The floor plan identifies all the locations of existing walls, electrical outlets, phone jacks, radiators, and anything else of this nature. The next step is to create the furniture plan, which drops pieces into the rooms once they've been defined. Together they give a complete picture.

A scaled floor plan on paper, to which you will later add cut-and-paste "virtual furniture," will allow you to decorate, demolish, and start again from scratch without ever moving so much as a footstool. This easily grasped and highly effective method (one of the most readily employed tools of design professionals) is only a tape measure and a pad of graph paper away.

Start with a basic rough sketch of your room. Include windows, doors, and heating units. For the moment, forget measurements; you're trying to establish a general map of the space to fill with precise measurements later. Make note of all access doors, built-in shelving, and closets that open into the space, as well as electrical, phone, and television wiring, as these will play a surprisingly important role in determining how you place your belongings (or rewire your room) when the furniture plan begins to take shape.

Once this map has been developed, you now have the ability to accurately measure the room and add in those dimensions to your plan. After you've measured, pencil in your numerical markings on the rough sketch. Measure twice—even if you think you got it right the first time. Even the best among us has delivered a six-foot-four-inch loveseat for a four-foot-six-inch window nook, so take the time to check your readings. Once your measurements are on paper, it's time to transfer your sketch to grid-ruled graph paper, which can be found at any art-supply store. This will help give your drawings the accuracy of a professional plan.

A scale drawing is one that indicates the scale at which a room's plan is reduced to fit on a piece of paper. Correspondingly, ⅛-inch graph paper is composed of ⅛-inch squares, each of which represents any measurement the renderer assigns it but is generally translated in terms of feet. In ¼-inch scale, ¼-inch equals one foot, ¼-inch scale, ¼-inch equals one foot, and so on. For your first time out, try to find ¼-inch ruled grid paper as it is easier to read and draw on.

FURNITURE PLAN

Now you're ready to draw scale paper models of your existing furniture, plus new pieces that you would like to add to each room. You'll need a pair of scissors and a pad of graph paper, the same scale as the one used for your scale drawing. From this, you can cut approximated shapes of your preexisting or wish-list furnishings. By placing the scaled cutouts into the floor plan you've just completed, you'll begin to understand the options and importance of furniture placement. Don't be afraid to use these cutouts to explore various seating arrangements. This is clearly the most economic way to define your decorative and functional goals.

Keep in mind when developing your plan that each room cannot operate independently of the others. Once you've developed a plan for each room, cut and paste these plans together to create a combined furniture and floor plan that shows the alignment of all the rooms in the house. Seen together, some of your decisions may change to create more practical traffic patterns that accommodate not only each room's function, but guide you gracefully into the adjoining space.

INSIDER TIPS

A good rule of thumb: leave about fifteen inches between a sofa and an occasional or coffee table, and no less than three feet of backup space behind chairs that face a desk or dining table. Here, the 1 + 1 = 3 rule applies: one person, taking one

THIS ROOM celebrates cultural diversity. The placement of an eighteenth century English chest with a Swedish chair and a contemporary steel side table enhances the unique qualities of each piece.

step, requires three feet to do it. Use your own visual logic and psychological comfort when setting up your rooms.

Less is not more. Most people believe that the less furniture you put in a room, the larger it will look. The opposite is true: rooms actually feel bigger with furniture in them than when they are empty. The more things your room is doing for you, the more opportunity you have to use it and take advantage of its appealing qualities. A room should be just as comfortable for twenty as it is for two, so try to build into it as many opportunities for private moments, perspectives, vistas as you can.

Once you've determined what plan is most comfortable for soft furniture and case goods, use it to develop electrical, lighting, communication, and sound system plans. This will make your house as functional as it is attractive.

Area rugs and carpets are critical to defining space. A single rug unites a space, two rugs can divide it, and three rugs will create a series of intimate furniture groupings.

CREATING A VISUAL PERSPECTIVE

Not every room in your house can be a room with a view. Never settle for a seating arrangement that offers only one perspective. The key is to make sure that you have set up furniture in such a way as to keep everything that's wonderful about your space as visible and accessible as possible. In the same way we thought about traffic movement between rooms, visual perspective or line of sight from one room to the other should also be considered. This means that what you see in the next room is as important as what you see in front of you.

Now that I've got you in the planning mode and creatively energized, it's time to experiment with a more imaginative furniture plan. Let's be a little daring and break the mold of those all-too-predictable symmetrical arrangements. People invariably want to center the sofa on the middle of the longest wall and then lock it in with a pair of chairs flanking it or, alternatively, anchor the same arrangement to a fireplace. You can have the right wall color, good-looking fabrics, and a

A well-designed room is equally attractive whether it's filled with many people or just one.

great carpet, but a doctor's-waiting-room furniture plan can destroy the whole scheme. Another inclination is to put all the furniture into one big circle in the middle of the room, thereby forfeiting the rest of the space and readying it for a rip-roaring group therapy session. The only thing that's missing is a box of Kleenex next to every chair. There's also the notion that there has to be an L-shaped relationship between pieces of furniture—one long sofa with a shorter one placed perpendicular to it, usually in the middle of the room. What people don't understand is that they've taken a nice-sized room and made it a small room, because everything around or behind that upholstered program becomes a passageway. For me, the goal has always been—no matter what size room I'm creating—to make it appear larger rather than smaller. I suggest you adopt the same goal.

What I want you to take away from this chapter is the great truth that furniture planning is about seeing rooms in a fresh way. Figure out how you can get two or three different uses out of a room, expanding its potential. A good place to start experimenting is the living room. It not only has the most potential of any room in the house, but it also has the reputation of being the most underutilized room. If you think outside the symmetrical box, you may find that you can have at least two different-sized sofas in the room instead of one that dominates the plan. An asymmetrical format will permit, I guarantee you, a minimum of two seating areas—one with a larger seating capacity, like an eight-foot sofa, and the other with a more intimate capacity, using a love seat or a six-foot sofa. By pushing everything away from the center of the room, you open it up. Correspondingly, these two disparate seating areas bring opportunity. If, for instance, there's space for a third location, you might try a games table and four small chairs, or perhaps a chaise lounge. By moving the large upholstered furniture to the perimeter of the room, you've opened up the core, adding lightness, personality, and dimension.

The point of great decoration is to explore new ideas, be open to suggestions, and enjoy the process of listening and learning. Best of all, furniture planning is a phase of the decorating process that requires no financial investment. There are no obligations. Borrow pieces from different rooms in the house to experiment, and just start pushing the furniture

THE SIMPLE INCLUSION of a low stool or ottoman in front of a coffee table helps to complete a conversational grouping. The goal here was to avoid using too many upholstered pieces.

around. You can always put the library sofa back in its place at the end of the day or decide, at long last, that it's actually better in its new location. Once you've reviewed these opportunities for a more creative—and ultimately more inviting—furniture plan, you can take the technique and expand it into the other rooms you would like to decorate. Now that you've attacked what you thought was the trickiest room in the house, the rest of your rooms will seem like small game. ■

HOW TO SELECT THE PERFECT TABLE:

Both the coffee and tea tables were designed to go in front of a sofa, but were meant to serve very different purposes.

Traditionally, a coffee (or cocktail) table should sit low to the ground in front of the sofa, almost crying out to be loaded up with books, a scented candle, and a bowl of nuts. Don't forget, they also make great ottomans, so do expect your family members to put their feet up when watching television. Therefore, make sure you choose a table made of durable or practical material.

The tea table was developed in the eighteenth century as a place from which to serve tea in the seated position (unlike its higher cousin, the dining table). Tea tables are usually between eighteen and twenty-three inches high, making them ideal for locations where you would like to have dinner away from the dining room—perhaps curled up on a sofa. It is still a great location for books, and it does double duty as a versatile small dining table. Two tea tables in front of a sofa are better than one.

5 | SCALE

Here's how I judge if I've been successful in designing a space: if someone calls up a client of mine and says, "Thanks for inviting me to the best dinner in years! The food was delicious and the house was so comfortable and beautiful." God help me if instead they say, "Wonderful party. Where did you get the chair?" If this should happen, I'll know I've failed because it will mean that I haven't been decorating, I've been shopping.

SCALE
CHAPTER FIVE

Successful decorating is about creating an intangible atmosphere that charms and beguiles. You can't tie it to one particular object; you just know you feel good in a particular space.

The overall effect of a room is achieved in large part through scale, and it's the manipulation of scale that gives us the impact we want in a room. Even if the objects themselves are not of extraordinary quality or great value, the act of putting something large next to something small or putting a beautifully curved chair next to a large rectilinear cabinet creates a visual dialogue that is pleasing to the eye. When we're

THIS IMAGE IS THE EMBODIMENT of an imaginative use of scale. The room's tall ceilings are emphasized by the totemlike Noguchi paper lantern. The wallpaper is applied in grid form which acts as a virtual ladder that connects the floor and ceiling.

SCALE CAN BE AS SIMPLE as choosing the right size candle. Notice how these thirty-two inch tapers dramatize the height of this partition wall (above). THE VERTICAL SCALE of these book towers is echoed by the column of photographs over the chair. Furniture, pictures, objects, and lighting all have the potential to make a contribution to the successful use of scale (right).

decorating we want to establish relationships between the objects in our space. It's the dialogue that helps to connect the dots throughout the room. By connecting the dots, I mean that each piece cannot exist on its own. It has to make a contribution to the piece next to it, and the one next to that. This contributes to the overall effect of a beautiful house. You want to walk in and notice the room, not the chair, or the lamp, or the painting.

The most mechanical way to understand scale is to learn to read a simple set of blueprints or plans. However, I've seen too many clients' eyes glaze over when I pull these out, so let's take a simpler approach that will help you get in tune with your

DO

DO think about your purchases. When you buy something, try to imagine how it will visually relate the objects around it.

DO be adventurous. Try putting your collection of toy soldiers next to the oversized glass bottle lamp.

DO remember that scale has the ability to enhance or diminish the intimacy of a room.

DO use the mantelpiece as the perfect stage to play with the scale of objects.

DO remember that the more diversity of color, texture, and scale, the more energetic and animated your rooms will be.

DO remember, great relationships of scale are absolutely free.

DON'T

DON'T buy it just because it's pretty.

DON'T let the size of your rooms unduly influence the size of the objects you put in them. Unlike clothes, rooms can accommodate objects of any size: small, medium, large, and extra-large.

DON'T start by hanging the picture over the sofa. First try it off to the side and low to the ground.

DON'T forget to judge the scale of your objects in the room from both the standing and seated positions.

sensory perception of space. Imagine yourself in a forest of very tall pine trees. How do you feel? Lonely? Comforted? Imagine yourself in a child's playhouse. Is it cozy or claustrophobic? This is your natural emotional response to scale. Let's take it a step further. If you like the feeling that you're in the forest on a walk and you like the majestic quality of tall trees, that's something you might want in your environment—the sense that the ceilings are higher and you have more space. If, however, you like it when you go to an intimate restaurant with dark ceilings, banquettes, and low candles on the table, that's a positive reaction to intimate scale and you may want your environment to envelop you.

In my own work, I try to play with scale. Just because you want an intimate space doesn't mean everything has to be small or low to the ground. If a majority of the things in your space

Scale creates a sense of wit, whimsy, and surprise. In other words, it creates personality.

are low and the space is dark, I suggest that you hang a huge painting. By introducing something of enormous scale, you will actually enhance the intimacy of the space. Balance is important. You won't appreciate what your intent is unless you have a point of reference.

When exploring scale, remember the importance of opposites. You cannot see a straight line unless there's a curved line to oppose it. If, for instance, you like large-scale objects and you want a lean, modern look, you might automatically think that instead of having a lot of objects, you should have one large table, such as a big refectory table or picnic table. But in order to appreciate the large scale of that object, you need something small to highlight it. Consider putting a dozen small Japanese bowls, in a row on that table. By mixing the two scales together you achieve the net result you sought.

If you enjoy grand scale, you might think you want grand furniture, but that's not necessarily so. Instead, choose lower furnishings to enhance the verticality of the space. That means a piece of furniture like a twelve-inch high Japanese cocktail table would be better than a twenty-eight-inch tea table, or a thirty-two-inch-high console. If you want the room to be intimate, almost cocoonlike, you can use larger furnishings, such as cabinetry or bookcases, which fill the space, bring the ceiling down, and promote the intimacy of the room.

When choosing furniture, what you should be looking for is diversity, because, as I've said, variation helps you appreciate scale. So, when thinking big, you must also think small. A coffee table is a classic example. Many people favor large ones piled high with books, flickering candles, and an orchid plant. It sounds wonderful, right? Now think about it. If you want a

THE LONG LOW chaise lounge in this bedroom further enhances the room's high ceilings. At the same time the relationship of chaise to table to plant lowers your sight line to establish intimacy (above). A "TABLESCAPE" is the perfect platform to reveal the endless possibilities of scale (right).

SCALE is simply the arrangement of objects in space. This Korean tansu, or storage cabinet, serves as a bedside table and helps you step up and into the room's scale.

big coffee table, and you want to dress it in the way I've described, don't start with a table that's already twenty-four inches off the ground. Instead start with one that's perhaps ten inches off the ground. Once you've added a stack of books and a tall plant, the table will visually be eighteen to twenty inches off the ground. All those tall objects will occupy the volume of space that you thought only the table should.

HEAR YOUR OWN DRUMMER   In chapter 4, I suggested you think outside the symmetrical box and become more imaginative when exploring and developing furniture plans. The same goes for scale. Don't buy into what everyone else has accepted just because you think you have to or you don't think you have any other options. It's understood that if you have a sofa in a room, you need a picture above it. But why not hang a picture low and to

It costs nothing to move objects around.

the side of your sofa? It will actually increase the sense of vertical scale in your room and give you something to look at when you're seated.

When decorating, people often judge the effectiveness of the room's scale by standing in its entryway. Wrong. The way you're going to use the room influences the scale of that space. For example, the scale in a living room should be addressed from the seated position. In the dining room, you might want

You can't see a straight
line unless there's a curved
line to oppose it.

to consider how it looks when you're standing at the door with a tray of food and when you're with your guests seated at the table. For a hallway, the movement of walking through space should determine the height of pictures and other objects you'll use to decorate.

The good news is that it doesn't cost money to resolve your scale issues. You can do it by rearranging—the same way that I suggested exploring furniture plans. Work with the objects you already have—it costs nothing to move them around into different places —and look at them for a day or two. Say you have three paintings, two chairs, a sofa, and a bookcase; those objects in and of themselves can give you four or five different reactions to the scale of the space. Change the setup every week for a few weeks in a row to give yourself a different perspective on where everything should be. All it takes is a little bit of time, your own curiosity, and a dash of daring.

Sometimes just placing a large object in a small space makes you appreciate the room. So again—be courageous. Mixing large objects with small ones is an energetic and animated use of space. The manipulation of scale fosters a sense of wit, whimsy, and surprise, but most important, it creates personality. ■

HOW TO FILL A BOOKCASE BEAUTIFULLY:

Bookcases, just like our furniture plan and the decorative objects we purchase, require some thought before installation. Frequently, I can redress a client's bookcase in little more than an afternoon and transform the appearance of the room without ever touching a chair. Here's how you can too.

If you're going to combine objects with books, don't randomly intermingle them. Set aside one shelf at the same location in all of your bookcases, and let that shelf be the stage for your growing collection of decoratives. Go one step further and paint the back of that display shelf a different color, perhaps dark brown, so the objects pop.

When filling your shelves with books, always bring the bindings of the books to the very front of the bookshelf, establishing a clear, clean, and edited straight line that brings an instant sense of order.

Negative space is important to scale as any other component. By leaving the wall above the sofa empty, and hanging the painting low and to the side, I emphasized the height of the room (above). When playing with scale in a bedroom, a clever solution is to have a canopy bed as high as possible. This is easily accomplished with a simple frame suspended from the ceiling and four panels of floor length-cloth (left).

BENJAMIN MOORE, ESSEX GREEN

TO CONNECT THE FURNITURE on this screened in porch leading to the garden, I dramatically lowered the height of the table and surrounded it with canoe chairs.

DON'T HESITATE to make bold moves when experimenting with paint. It's the most economical solution for dramatic change.

paint it an entirely different color.

Your hesitation may be a result of your indecision about what colors you actually want to experiment with. If that's the obstacle, begin defining what tones you like by looking at objects and items currently surrounding you. A good place to start is, as I mentioned in chapter 3, your own wardrobe. If you

The painting process is not about the paint, but the preparation.

find that the bulk of your clothing is ivory and tan or other warm colors, you might like to have those tones in your house. At the supermarket, are you drawn to the color of certain fruits and vegetables? Open up your senses and lose your inhibitions. Let's face it: whether it's painting your house or selecting a sweater, we make choices about color every day.

COLOR SELECTION

A frequently asked question regarding paint is: how can you pick a color from a paint chip that's the size of a postage stamp? The simple answer is: You can't. Paint stores are never going to tell you this, but it's nearly impossible to judge a color by what you see in the can or on the sample card. There is, however, a way to find the color you like without purchasing your seventy-fifth gallon. Many paints are available in quarts—buy several quarts of the colors that appeal to you.

PAINT WAS USED TO FURTHER the architecture of this hallway. The large, horizontal bands reference the architectural equivalent of blocks.

Then go to your local craft store and buy a dozen twenty by thirty-inch poster boards and give them two coats of paint each. Do two or three sheets for each color. Next, put the sheets in different locations in the same room. This will give you the opportunity to see how the color reacts to light: close to a window or deep in shadow, under a lamp, or by candlelight. This is much more important than most people think. Whether you're working with subtle pastels or bolder, more saturated tones, you're looking for colors with secondary characteristics—an afterglow or a quality that inexplicably becomes more appealing on the wall than it was in the can. It's almost impossible to recognize these traits from a swatch, but you will notice them immediately once you've seen the paint on your wall.

I recommend buying more than one shade of a color you think you like. You'll be amazed at how different they look on the walls. For instance, mint green has dozens of variables, so pick two or three. The minimum color selection should be three, and you can certainly do as many as five—let your excitement level guide you. Be sure to place the test boards in at least three or four locations. Over the next several days, set aside a few minutes to observe the color boards at three different times of the day. I guarantee that you'll be amazed at the efficiency of this deceptively simple technique. Don't be surprised if the winning color isn't the one that jumps off the wall at first glance. Often, it's the color that works on us subtly and draws us in at odd moments as we rush past it or glance up at it from our reading. When selecting colors, it's also important to think about what a particular room needs to do for you and what its message is. For example, if you have a big

Great decoration means you are tempted in every direction as you move through space.

If I had to name one decorating decision that people agonize over more than any other, it would be, hands down, what color to paint their rooms. The important thing to remember is that color is the most easily altered of all the decorative elements, so no mistake is permanent. Best of all, color is the quickest, most powerful, and most economical way to transform your house. Painting a room should be approached with a sense of liberation rather than trepidation.

THE POWER OF PAINT
CHAPTER SIX

Some paints are better for some things than others, but they all accomplish the same result: they change our perception of the rooms we live in. The great joy of color and paint is that they give us the opportunity to be both creative and thrifty at the same time. They also give us one of the greatest luxuries of all: the luxury of choice. A gallon of paint ranges in price from $15 to $50 a gallon. If you paint your library the garnet red you had fantasized about for years but six months later discover that you hate it, you can, for a couple hundred dollars,

THE SPLASH OF RED in the painting was a jumping off point for the red lacquer table. Whether it's furniture or walls, look for visual clues in your surroundings when choosing color for your rooms.

BENJAMIN MOORE, RAINFOREST DEW, 2146-50

WHEN WORKING with subtle colors, it's critical to test them in different levels of light. This room looks completely different, but
just as beautiful, by night as by day.

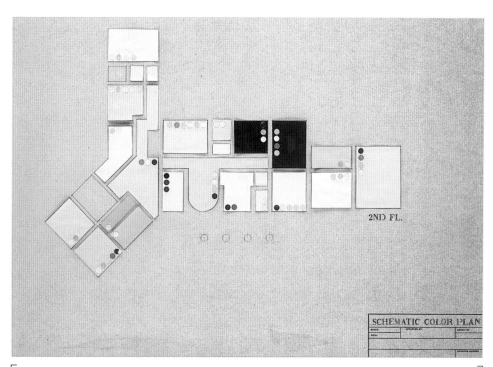

IN A LARGE RESIDENTIAL PROJECT I always develop a color chart that shows the principle color of each room and its coordinating palette for furniture. This is a useful tool for any scale project (above). THESE DARKLY PAINTED WALLS in a New York City restaurant are a powerful example of the importance of careful preparation of surfaces. The brown gloss is an ideal backdrop for the textured straw upholstery on the white chair frames (left).

house in the country with a large entryway, you might want to try a warm shade like burnt yellow or tawny brown to convey comfort and a sense of age upon entering. In an urban apartment you may want a cool, frosty shade in the entrance hall to promote an air of urban glamour. Whatever the environment, color establishes an emotional response and helps create the mood.

PREPARATION

Once you've selected your color, the most important part of the painting process is not the painting itself, but the preparation. Even if the walls are in good shape, I strongly advise that you spend the few extra bucks for a good quality

It's impossible to judge
a color by what you see in
the can or in the paint chip.

THE RIGHT WHITES

WE ALL KNOW THAT THE REAL KEY TO GREAT DECORATING IS SENSITIVITY. ONE OF THE GREATEST EXERCISES IN DECORATIVE SENSITIVITY IS THE CAREFUL SELECTION OF WHITE PAINT. WHO WOULD HAVE THOUGHT THAT THE ABSENCE OF ALL COLOR WOULD RESULT IN SO MANY CHOICES?

PLEASE NOTE: ALL PAINT COLORS ARE MANUFACTURED BY BENJAMIN MOORE.

DECORATOR'S WHITE #04 One of the few places where decoration is driven almost entirely by function is the closet interior. Don't be tempted to match them with the room color, which could alter or distort your vision of your wardrobe colors. Stick with this pure white.

ATRIUM WHITE #79 Ninety percent of the ceilings on my projects are painted this color. It's a clear white with a pink blush that's flattering to any wall color. Another refreshingly cool hit. Believe it or not, this color is perfect for a bedroom. It enhances your skin's natural pigment.

WHITE WATER BAY #0C70 For those of us who prefer all white rooms, this is the color that warms them up.

LAMBSKIN #0C3 Surprise! This is what I use on the other ten percent. If you follow my suggestion and paint your library or dining room a dark color, this is the color you'll want for your ceiling.

BONE WHITE READY-MIXED This is my biggest secret weapon. It's indispensable for painting doors. The subtle combination of this color against crisp white trim adds dramatic definition and depth to all conditions.

FOG MIST #0C31 The ideal workhorse. This is the white you want for utilitarian spaces like the laundry room, garage, or attic.

THINK ABOUT PLAYING with contrast in the paints you choose. Deep hues paired with whites or neutrals will add crispness to your colors (right). FOR THIS BEACH HOUSE, I made a statement by painting the floor in bands of blue and white. It has all the visual pleasure of carpet but without the maintenance (next page).

THE COLORS I LOVE

ALTHOUGH DESIGNERS ARE EXPECTED TO BRING A FRESH APPROACH AND A NEW PERSPECTIVE TO EACH PROJECT, THERE ARE INVARIABLY SOME INDUSTRY STANDARDS THAT NEVER FAIL. AFTER TWENTY YEARS IN THE DESIGN FIELD I HAVE DEVELOPED A PORTFOLIO OF PAINT COLORS ON WHICH I CONTINUALLY RELY.

PLEASE NOTE: ALL PAINT COLORS ARE MANUFACTURED BY BENJAMIN MOORE.

RAINFOREST DEW #2146-50
Cool tones like this green can be very flattering on walls. This color makes the perfect background for an elegantly appointed living room.

HARBOR FOG #2062-70
Another refreshingly cool hit. Believe it or not, this color is perfect for a bedroom. It flatters your skin's natural pigment.

MOONLIGHT #2020-60
Children's rooms are, far too often, painted childlike colors. Why not fill them with sunlight and optimism?

MELLOW YELLOW #2020-60
This is a color that has been used far too frequently in bedrooms. As it happens, it's a much better shade to greet you in the breakfast room.

YELLOW HAZE #2017-50
Invariably, staircases and hallways are the gloomiest rooms in the house because they get little or no natural daylight. Bright pastels like this one conquer those negatives.

EDGECOMB GRAY #HC-173
If your ceilings are lower than eight feet, a pure white ceiling paint can only serve to remind you of this condition. A pale gray such as this one will make the ceiling appear higher.

GRANT BEIGE #HC-83
This color is ideal for painting interior woodwork on houses near an ocean or a lake. Why? Because pure white is simply too harsh.

ALEXANDRIA BEIGE #HC-77
Perfect for a living room. Imagine how your furniture and objects will pop against this background.

JAVA #2106-10
A medium-to-dark brown is ideal in assisting us to focus. This one is just right for a study or a home office.

BLACK BEAN SOUP #2130-10
Don't even think about painting your library any other color until you see this first.

GENTLEMAN'S GRAY #2062-20
An elegant nighttime color. Imagine how beautiful your dining room will be if done in this color in high gloss.

ESSEX GREEN #43 EXTERIOR READY-MIXED
What you see on the outside of a house is a hint of the decorative pleasure within. This is a classic for shutters.

primer. This is where most people skimp, because they think no one will ever see it. In fact, a great primer sets the stage for a great application of paint. This is particularly true if your walls have imperfections; the better the primer, the less the paint is absorbed into the walls, which means you're going to spend less money on the paint itself.

If your walls or woodwork have cracks or imperfections that simply won't disappear no matter the prep work, don't lose sleep over it. Hit those areas with the best paint you can afford and remember that strategically placed furniture and paintings will disguise many of these flaws. The goal of painting is to move your decorating process forward, not slow you down.

OPPOSITES ATTRACT

A designer friend of mine always says, "The best thing about a beige living room is an aubergine dining room." He's absolutely right. Juxtaposing colors creates a dialogue. When a client says to me, "I want pink!" the first thing I'll produce is a blue paint chip, because that's what makes pink look dazzling. Every house or apartment should read like a story, with each part clearly defined and connected to the next in a sequence that leads you through with pizzazz. Color, more than anything else, is your faithful guide, and it helps to repeat certain color details from room to room, even as you change the body of the wall color. For example, in one house I worked on, the dining room had a chair rail—known as the dado—and I painted the wall underneath a dark, glossy bottle green. The living room, separated by the entry, also had a chair rail and dado. While the wall colors of the rooms were different shades of yellow, I used the same bottle green on the dado in each room. The goal was to unify the rooms by directing the eye to both spaces. I wanted to make both rooms equally alluring because they are right off an entrance that's painted a strong orange. The point is, one room shouldn't take precedence over the other. Great decoration means that you are tempted in every direction as you move through space.

The downfall of not listening to your inner decorative voice is that there's always one room that you'll consistently gravitate toward because that's where you've spent the most money and energy. The other rooms end up weak and virtually unused because less thought has gone into them. Make sure that your decoration inspires you to use all the rooms in your house. A dining room shouldn't be reserved for holiday meals. The living room shouldn't be used just for formal entertaining, rendering the kitchen the heart and soul of the house. To prevent these things from happening you need a visual unifier that tempts you into the spaces, and that visual unifier is paint.

WHISPER OR SHOUT

On another note, paint can also be used to create drama or metaphorical exclamation points in a house. People are often terrified by the thought of painting a room with a dark or bold color. They tend to think it will make the space too dramatic. Don't be scared. In fact, the perception of a dark space can be much different than its reality. By painting a room dark brown or green, your eye is going to be drawn to the lightness within the room's components. On page 121, you'll see a living room painted ebony brown—so dark it actually looks black. However, the room doesn't seem dark at all. Your eye is immediately drawn to the white sofa and the white matting of the printed ferns hanging on the wall. This room appears to be filled with light, thanks to the contrast of the dark paint with the light furnishings. It's dramatic but livable. Drama doesn't have to mean that you use color as a theatrical event and then sit in the audience. It means that the shade will enhance the satisfaction you get out of using the room. Color serves a purpose.

I'm often asked to suggest the best paint color for rooms that don't get much sunlight. My answer is always the same: the purpose of the room will help to establish your color. If it's a library or a dining room, it's not necessarily a bad thing that it's dark. In fact, that may be an asset. These rooms are used for inward-facing experiences, and a dark color can amplify a mood of reflection.

The rewards of color and paint are not limited to walls. You may be satisfied with what's already on them and looking for a way to perk up a particular room. If that's your goal, try painting a piece of furniture whose shape you like. A simple change like repainting that dark wood table a crisp white or bright red will transform the space instantly. Or consider painting your floor, which has the potential to do more for a room than repainting your walls. Unexpected color can be as much a part of the decoration as the furniture itself. Think of paint as an object, not just a background.

CONTRARY TO POPULAR BELIEF, dark painted walls can actually lighten rooms provided you introduce a healthy dose of cream, ivory, or white.

7 | MATERIAL
CONCERNS

When we think about the materials that are

used for decoration, we think of paint, paper, and fabric. In fact, these are just the beginning. While you can make a statement with paint, paper, and fabrics, there are other elements you can incorporate that will add personality to your space. Take, for instance, curtain rods. Instead of the painted or polished-wood variety, think about using Lucite tubing or oxidized iron. And what are the options when it comes to the surface of a door? Don't limit yourself to painted wood. The door could be upholstered leather and covered in nail heads like one you might see in Morocco. Or why not completely clad in mirror?

MATERIAL CONCERNS

CHAPTER SEVEN

GONE BUT NOT FORGOTTEN

We often overlook the materials that surround us. Plastic laminate, for example, is usually relegated to kitchen and bathroom cabinets. But does that mean you can't use it to make furniture? Actually,

THIS ROOM is all about layering. Mixing the linen velvet sofa with the tortoise shell occasional table, blue linoleum floor, and satin-covered gilded chair creates a rich living space, where lucky visitors can bask in a feast for the senses.

laminate makes a Parson's table or coffee table, which is both attractive and perfect for a house with small children. There's a beauty to recognizing the honesty and integrity of basic materials by putting them to an unexpected use. Lucite is another favorite. Anyone can find a fourteen-inch square Lucite box at a plastic store. This material often has a negative connotation because of its association with mid-1970s decoration.

My firm has reinvented Lucite by sandblasting it, which makes it opaque. These cubes are a hallmark of our style and are easily reproduced. Just consult your yellow pages for a sandblaster, and you're in business.

On the other hand, nature provides numerous materials that can be used decoratively. A favorite of mine is firewood. I've used it to create walls for outdoor terraces and loggias that act as a wind buffer in the early fall or spring, making it both practical and imaginative. I've also taken a dozen pieces of firewood, stood them on end, and bundled them together to create rustic side tables.

PRIVACY, PLEASE

The joy of materials comes from their thoughtful use. Don't be limited by preconceived notions. Curtains don't have to be used only at the windows, but instead can also be used to partition space. Instead of using a door to close off a room, consider mounting a track or rod on the ceiling and draping material from it. You can vary the effect by using different kinds of materials. If you want a dense and opaque barrier, try

FOR THIS KITCHEN I stripped off the paint to reveal the original steel cabinetry. I like the honesty of returning materials to their natural state.

velvet. If you would like to allow light through, try a gossamer theatrical scrim, which will give a sense of intimacy and enclosure when drawn without blocking light.

You may have a room that will no longer have windows after

You don't have to go back to square one to get what you want.

you've put up a partition. Building a solid wall with Sheetrock would create a dark, airless space. If, however, it were made of a solid yet translucent material like sandblasted glass, it would give you light as well as privacy. Venetian blinds as a room separator are another unconventional alternative to solid walls. Blinds allow you to enclose space and to permit light and air to circulate when needed.

WALL COVERING

When it comes to wall surfaces there are a variety of options to choose from that go beyond paint and paper. When we hear the word *wallpaper*, visions of awning stripes or giant flower patterns spring to mind. A more updated approach is to look for something that lends texture and body to the walls, such as grass cloth or a coarse linen wall covering. If you're feeling really inspired, take a trip to your local art store. There you'll find a selection of interesting artist's papers, such as bookbinder's vellum, parchment, or heavily textured watercolor paper. Even simple tissue paper makes a beautiful wall surface. Simply paint the walls your favorite color, then apply white or colored tissue paper with latex adhesive using a large brush. The tissue paper will become semitransparent, adding texture and body to the painted surface. Another favorite trick of mine is to use metallic paper in spaces where there is limited light, such as entrance halls, bathrooms, and often dining rooms. The paper both reflects and softens light.

Fabric is another alternative for your walls. There was a time when people were indulgent and loved the idea of doing luxurious padded or upholstered walls. If you like the idea of using fabric, you don't have to invest the time and expense of fattening it up with heavy padding. The point is to add a level of quality to the room. So, if you like the fabric on your sofa, there's no reason that you can't simply put adhesive on the back and apply it to the wall. If you're worried about how the seams align, just marry the selvage ends edge to edge, then apply a decorative tape or a half bamboo rod over the seam. It doesn't have to be elaborate to achieve a beautiful result. You also don't have to use expensive upholstery-weight cloth, though it is much more durable. Dressmaker's fabric is another alternative—one that you can buy for as little as a few dollars a yard—and is often less expensive than standard rolls of wallpaper. This technique is not something to attempt on your own: a

THE FORGOTTEN MATERIALS

MORE OFTEN THAN NOT, WE GRAVITATE TOWARD COMMONLY USED MATERIALS IN OUR DECORATING. SO WHEN MY CLIENTS ASK ME TO SUGGEST MATERIALS, I ALWAYS TRY TO OFFER UNEXPECTED CHOICES THAT ARE VISUALLY EFFECTIVE YET STILL PRACTICAL. HERE ARE A FEW FAVORITES:

LAMINATES ON TABLES:
This material continues to evolve in color, finish, and price, therefore providing a wide range of options.

KITCHEN COUNTERTOPS CAST IN POLISHED CONCRETE:
The great beauty of concrete is its ability to absorb different colors and finishes.

UNLINED CURTAINS AS ROOM DIVIDERS INSTEAD OF SOLID WALLS:
They allow light in but still provide privacy.

TISSUE PAPER FOR WALLS:
Tissue paper is the most affordable material to add texture to ho-hum construction and the most fun to apply—Elmer's Glue, water, and a paint brush will do the job.

FIREWOOD AS EXTERIOR WALLS:
Instead of enclosing your porch in glass why not opt for a natural wind barrier that protects you during the cold season. Firewood does the job and also lends a natural beauty to the space.

CARPET IN THE BATHROOM:
Why ruin the luxury of a warm shower by stepping out onto a cold floor?

CORK IN THE KITCHEN:
This is the material that time forgot. In the early 1900s, cork flooring was preferred for domestic kitchens and remains to this day the choice of professional chefs in restaurant kitchens.

BAMBOO FLOORS:
This material is half the price of standard wood flooring yet it's visually exotic and spare at the same time. It's also temperature-stable, meaning it never gets hot or cold based on climate.

METAL BOOKCASES:
When people hear the word bookcase, they invariably think of wood. Metal is an attractive and diverse alternative with finishes ranging from rough sanded to waxed to painted.

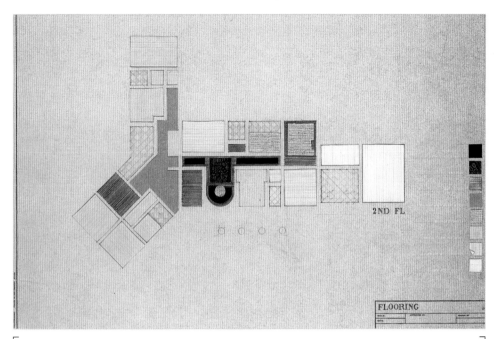

I ALWAYS DEVELOP a chart that helps me understand how options for floor materials and their coverings relate to one another as you move through the house (above). FOR AN ENTRANCE HALL that has no natural light, materials that reflect light are crucial. Here, I used silver leaf paper on the ceiling, mirror on the walls and polished linoleum on the floor (left).

qualified wallpaper hanger is highly recommended.

In addition to being beautiful, wall coverings have a practical advantage over paint. Grass cloth, unrefined paper, and fabric are forgiving materials. You can drive nails in and out of them if you're changing or rehanging pictures, and you won't see the nail hole because the overall pattern and texture of the paper helps to disguise it. You're mistaken if you think you can do the same thing in a painted room without having to replaster and repaint. In this way, fabric and textured wallpapers also encourage you to be more creative and spontaneous in the way that you live, because you can move items around freely without worrying about the maintenance a flat-painted wall demands.

Don't look at wall covering solely as a material to add decoration. Rather, look at it as something that will also add integrity

BENJAMIN MOORE, ALEXANDRIA BEIGE, HC-77

CURTAINS IN THIS HALLWAY are unlined linen that captures the natural daylight and gives it a translucent quality. The material you select for curtains can actually enhance light rather than detract from it.

Even the humblest
of materials can be
ennobled by design.

PALACES OF FLORENCE

to your rooms and give them a personality and patina. One of the biggest obstacles in decorating today is the lack of character in new construction. No matter how much decorating you do to give your home definition, the house or the apartment still doesn't seem to have the depth, or the dignity, or the substance you want. Where paint simply glides over the surface of a wall, leaving it sterile, textured wallcoverings like grass cloth and fabric visually bond to the wall and lend dimension.

The materials that decorators use today are diverse and imaginative. There's a new interest in taking formerly utilitarian spaces like the kitchen and bathroom and modifying them to be more comfortable. As a result, more of these spaces are lined with wall coverings. It's no longer a given that you have to tile an entire bathroom. If you're laying out tiles for a recently renovated bathroom, use the tiles strategically, placing them only in areas that could get wet (for example, outside the shower or around the sink). Again, I encourage you to think imaginatively. Perhaps your bathroom would look great if you covered the remaining wall in woven straw cloth, which is sold by the roll and is similar to sisal or burlap; some are now made of vinyl or rubber and will withstand steam. Don't stop there. After you've changed the surface, enhance the effect by hanging copies of treasured photographs or drawings to further domesticate the room. (Don't use original photos, as they can be damaged by moisture. Make copies instead.)

Another example of the changing attitudes toward kitchens and bathrooms can be found underfoot. For instance, you'll often see a house with a beautiful wooden floor that stops

THE SELECTION OF MATERIALS can also redirect light into a room. The pewter leaf wall covering captures the light from an unseen window and softly moves it into the space.

when it reaches the entrance to a kitchen, the floor of which people felt compelled to tile or otherwise cover with an impervious material, such as vinyl. Let me tell you, a tile or linoleum floor is unnecessary. Why not extend the existing wood floors from the adjoining rooms? It will visually unify the space and demilitarize the kitchen zone.

IT IS WHAT IT IS

Often we're faced with unattractive preexisting materials in our houses that are costly to rip out and replace. Tiled floors in bathrooms are a common problem. An easy, luxurious, and affordable solution is to install wall-to-wall carpet—right over the tile. No one ever said we couldn't carpet our bathrooms, did they? What you need to know is that the carpet shouldn't be installed with the traditional method of glue or tacks. Instead, have the carpet cut to fit and the edges bound, and lay it over the tile. You can easily remove the carpet if you need to have it cleaned.

Kitchens are another area where distasteful existing materials may lead us to think we need to renovate. Hold on a second! Before you rip out cabinetry because you don't like the color, look to see what's underneath. Perhaps what's lurking under the paint is something far more pleasing and much less expensive than the new units you fell in love with at the kitchen showroom. If you live in an old house or a prewar apartment, you might find wonderful oak or 1930s steel cabinets that can be stripped to reveal the splendor of the original material. And just because your woodwork is cherry doesn't mean it has to stay that way or be replaced: most woods can be stained a variety of colors that have nothing to do with their original material. In a kitchen or any room where you have built-in cabinetry, never accept the idea that you're stuck with what's there.

Another design dilemma for homeowners today is the purchase of a house or apartment that's been recently built or newly decorated by a previous owner whose taste doesn't jibe with their own. In essence, you're shelling out money for details you dislike, and typically they're expensive features, such as flooring or bath fixtures. If it pains you to throw out what you've paid for, there are solutions. I've worked with many a marble floor that was inappropriate to its location. Instead of worrying about the cost of removing it, I made a conscious decision to simply cover that area with a more humble material like an area rug made from a material like sisal or jute. I then leave an eight- or twelve-inch border of the stone at the outside edge. Or maybe it has to be wall-to-wall carpeting even though you

Consider the things you love in your daily life: a favorite sweater, or antique porcelain vase.

were hoping for hardwood. At least the carpet hides the condition that you find unattractive, and it's a much more economical solution than ripping the existing floor out.

Similarly, there's nothing to prevent you from painting or papering marble, granite, or stone walls. I've encountered bathrooms with inappropriate stone walls and I've wallpapered right over them. Paper adheres just as easily to stone as

THIS SKETCH proves that selecting dark floors can successfully direct your eye to the forms and furnishings of a room (above). THE CLIENTS' COLLECTION OF VINTAGE RECORDS became a valuable visual tool in the decorative program. Instead of relegating them to the closet, we designed a bookcase to emphasize them. Sometimes materials or objects can transcend their original purpose (left).

it does to gypsum board. It's comforting to know that you don't have to go back to square one to get what you want.

As for objectionable kitchen and bathroom fixtures, try to decide whether it's the shape or the finish that you hate. If it's the shape, you might have to invest in something new. But if you can live with the shape of the faucet or the tap handle, simply disconnect the fixtures and send them out to a metal shop—even an auto repair shop will do—and have them replated in the finish of your choosing: pewter, satin, nickel, or gunmetal. The sky's the limit.

When clients come to me for an initial meeting to help me define what their goals and needs are—or what their likes and dislikes are—I always tell them not to worry about bringing me tear sheets from magazine articles about other people's houses. Instead, I tell them to bring me samples of things from their daily life that they love. Many times, I'll learn more from a cashmere shawl, a piece of porcelain, or a well-worn pair of suede gloves than I will from a picture of a house that is unattainable. I've had people come in with just a beautiful Chinese ceramic bowl because they like the colors, or a favorite sweater because they like the texture. That doesn't mean I'm going to upholster their chair in sweaters. It means we're going to take that information and find

HOW TO MEASURE A ROOM FOR AN AREA RUG:

This one is a no-brainer. Simply decide whether you want the furniture to sit on or off the area rug.

If your desired goal is on, measure the room in both directions and subtract two feet from each direction. This means that if the room is ten by fourteen feet, the perfect area rug is eight by twelve. Allowing one foot of polished wood flooring exposed in any direction is generally considered a successful relationship of carpet to wood.

If off is your desire, which obviously exposes more flooring, find the largest piece of furniture in the room that's against any wall. Add one inch to the depth of that piece to calculate the amount of exposed border required at the other walls. For instance, if your chest of drawers is twenty-three inches deep, you will require a twenty-four inch exposed border along all four walls. Therefore, if the room is ten by fourteen feet, the perfect area rug is six by ten feet.

140

materials that are complementary to that texture. I urge you to try this. It's a great way to understand materials and how you respond to them.

MATERIALS TALK When exploring materials, however, you still have to be sensitive to the environment in which you'll be using them. Trends often facilitate an inappropriate use of materials. In my opinion, a popular trend that lasted far too long was the idea of creating an English country house decorating scheme in urban apartments. Personally, I think it's more modern to use materials that are indigenous to where you live. For a country environment, you want materials that are friendlier, a little more timeworn. For the city, I think you want to use more sophisticated materials, perhaps elements that are sleeker or a little more glamorous. When selecting materials, always consider where and how they will be used, and what contribution they make on a decorative level. ▪

TAKING MATERIALS OUT OF CONTEXT can provide great creative solutions. Here the mirrored chest of drawers was turned into a bathroom sink.

8 | OBSTACLE
OR OPPORTUNITY?

Now that I've covered the basic steps you'll need to take to decorate your home, it's time to address some common wrinkles that you may encounter during the process. Often in the middle of working on a project, my design team and I are confronted with a column in the wrong place, an ill-proportioned window, or a deeply ugly upholstered chair that a client loves but we don't. These issues encourage and motivate us to be more creative as designers. In reality, it's a small percentage of homeowners who have the luxury of changing unattractive preexisting conditions. The cost of renovation, whether it's urban or rural, is skyrocketing daily. Luckily, many problems that seem insurmountable can be overcome by thinking decoratively. And, more often than not, these creative solutions are more successful, and certainly more economical, than renovation.

So before we continue with our design tutorial, let's focus on a few classic examples of less than perfect preexisting features.

OBSTACLE OR OPPORTUNITY?
CHAPTER EIGHT

SOMETIMES A ROOM can seem too big. By placing bookcases in the middle of this one, I created two intimate spaces where none existed previously.

Believe it or not, there are ways to turn something around without having to gut it, pitch it, or donate it to charity.

How we do make a low ceiling look like it has some height? Let's start with the simplest solution: painting your ceiling with good quality high-gloss paint. Glossy paint reflects the light, creating a vertical illusion and making your eye perceive the ceiling to be higher than it really is.

Architectural additions and details can also make a room appear taller. This doesn't necessarily mean adding a detail where the wall meets the ceiling. In fact, the opposite is true. Instead of emphasizing the ceiling and its relationship to the wall, emphasize your baseboard. Most new structures have a baseboard no higher than three inches—if there's one at all. I suggest making a much larger one. That can be as simple as installing a twelve-inch-high, one-inch-thick plank of wood all the way around the room. By adding a significant architectur-

Decorative fixes are often more successful—and certainly less expensive—than renovation.

al detail at the baseboard, you lower your sight line. It's up to you how much more you want to embellish it. You could, for instance, buy two or three stock baseboards and stack them

IT DOESN'T REQUIRE A HAMMER and a saw to make architectural changes. By closing off these double doors and placing a table and mirror in front of them, I created a welcoming entryway for this country house.

DREARY HALLWAYS can be turned into dramatic passageways. For this one, I curtained the walls and furthered the dramatic affect by placing a mirror at the end thereby doubling its impact.

together to create significantly more architectural detail. This trick will visually increase the height of the room by a third simply by emphasizing the weight at the bottom of the room, making the upper part of the room feel lighter and more airy.

If you're determined to have a traditional flourish of molding in a low-ceilinged space, try this next trick: instead of applying the standard crown molding to the wall, place a six-inch-wide, one-inch-thick plank directly on the ceiling. Paint it the same flat white as the ceiling itself, establishing the visual effect of a stepped plaster tray. You will have accomplished your goal without reducing your wall space.

Another solution to low ceilings is to remove the header

from any or all doors in the room. A header is the area of the wall above the door between the frame and the ceiling. Removing it will give you more than a feeling of height; it will transform the way you enter that room and the way you perceive the room itself. More often than not, there is no structural reason that a door has to be the height it is (usually seven to seven and a half feet). It's only that height because the builder has been doing every house or apartment the exact same way for the last twenty years. Don't assume that builders have valid reasons for what they do; sometimes they just want to get the project done.

If you're going to create a new opening, here's what you do to make it look finished. Remove the molding from the top of the door frame, leaving the sides intact, and raise the door opening all the way up to the ceiling. Then, extend the molding on either side of the door frame up to the ceiling. What you will end up with is a ceiling that rolls right through your space from room to room. This is not labor intensive: a couple hours of painless demolition by you or your handyman will provide a long-lasting sense of architectural sincerity and excitement to your room.

CEILING BEAMS   Another easily solved problem is a haphazardly placed cross beam. A cross beam is the beam that traverses a room on the ceiling, usually designating its ability to support the structure above. Even if the beam serves a structural purpose, it often doesn't have even the remotest geometric relationship to the room. The immediate response is to throw your

BENJAMIN MOORE, EDGECOMB GRAY, HC-173

THIS PHOTO illustrates the successful use of a stepped ceiling.

Design obstacles
are nothing more than
opportunities.

hands up in the air and look the other way.

When I'm confronted with an ill-proportioned but structurally required cross beam, I create what's called a reflected ceiling plan. Essentially this means that I draw what I would see if I were looking straight up at the ceiling, which will help me visualize where the beam falls within the room. If I then add a mirror image of the existing beam on the opposite side of the room, I justify the existing beam. The goal is to create symmetry and the end result is a beautiful beamed ceiling that you didn't have before. You can carry the idea further by adding two more cross beams to create a coffered ceiling, which could be even more attractive. We've all seen those but perhaps you don't know it by name. A coffered ceiling is a grid of beams between which are raised panels commonly known as coffers. With a couple of swift design decisions, a little bit of sheet rock, some framing, and a bucket of paint, you've transformed an obstacle into something that adds more depth and interest to the room.

SUPPORT COLUMNS

Many rooms have one or more columns that support the ceiling. Often these columns are in awkward places because they're functional, not decorative. If you are faced with an oddly placed support column, you can add another column to the same location on the opposite wall, making a mirror image of the existing one. This solution is similar to the one I suggested for the awkwardly placed ceiling beam. You are creating symmetry. You can then dress up the columns in the decorative style of your choice.

Depending on the size and shape of your room, your new pair of columns can also divide the space, so instead of one big room, you might appreciate the possibility of having two small sitting rooms that share a common passageway defined by the columns. Or, if that pesky existing column is at the entrance to the room—for example, three or four feet from the doorway—adding another column is a great way to establish a sense of arrival. If your front door opens directly into the living room, you can create a formal entrance or foyer by adding two sets of columns to your entryway.

This is another relatively easy way to add beauty to your home, but if you're fearful of making a drastic mistake, the columns are easy to mock up. Take a few yards of cloth, form it into a hollow column, and suspend it from the ceiling to simulate the extra column. You can also use a column of books or a stack of boxes.

WINDOWS

Standard-size windows are a common problem. My clients long for larger windows, especially in the living room and dining room, where elegance is desired. You could replace your small windows with French or triple-hung versions, which would give you the elongated form you're seeking. Unfortunately, replacing windows is a costly operation, and it can lead to a frenzy of spending. The next thing you know, you're replacing the shutters, re-shingling the house, and re-pouring the foundation. Luckily, there are simpler solutions.

Perhaps the best place to start is not with the window itself, but how it has been dressed—either with curtains, shutters, or shades. Changing the treatment can dramatically enhance the impact of your windows. When it comes to curtains, one of the most common mistakes people make is to put the curtain rod at the top of the window frame instead of at the top of the wall where the crown molding begins. Place the rod up as high as you possibly can above the window frame and let the curtains drop to the floor. This will instantly make the windows look taller and more elegant without altering the existing conditions. If you want to further enhance the size of your windows, add a painted panel to the wall above and below the window. This is a significant architectural addition without a significant financial investment. The panel—done in the same color as your window trim, preferably white—provides a visual link between the baseboard and the crown molding.

If you have an unstoppable urge to replace ugly windows, I suggest that you first take a look at the ones in your bathroom or powder room. For some unknown reason, someone got it into his or her head to install Lilliputian windows in these spaces. Many times, these windows are a significantly ugly aspect of the house as a whole because they also ruin the façade. Replacing such a window is a great opportunity to make a positive change. After all, we spend a good amount of time in these rooms, so why not make them attractive? And don't rule out a different shape. Changing a standard rectangular window to a porthole or a much larger window could well provide the architectural beauty you're seeking.

WRESTLING WITH A LARGE HIGH-END STEREO SPEAKER was a challenge. Rather than fight it, I let its graphic quality influence the fabric for the chair next to it. The speaker now provides a sculptural addition to the decorative solution.

Obviously, one can't donate that nasty support column or unsightly cross beam to the local church charity, but certainly more than its fair share of upholstered furniture has mysteriously shown up on many a church doorstep. Before you, too, are tempted to make that midnight drop, let's look at your options. First, consider the form of your furniture. If you like the essential shape of your furniture, you can save a pot of money. More times than I can remember, I've been called in by my clients who have at long last taken an objective look at their twenty years' worth of accumulated upholstery and recoiled at the autobiographical mess before them. Remember that rolled-arm plaid sofa you had to have? What about those years you went French, followed quickly by your English period, which was just moments before you discovered feng shui? The trick is to get past the period statements your furniture upholstery makes and look at the shapes of the individual

Start with the simplest solution.

pieces. Obviously, some furniture shapes will be more compatible with others. Try to group your furniture by complementary shapes, eliminating pieces that don't relate. Once you've done that, you're ready to consider some solutions to the plaid-floral-baroque frenzy that's in front of you.

THE MAJOR OBSTACLE in this entry, which feeds directly into the living room, was the electrical panel box located in the center of the entrance. Unable to move it, I built a column that became a point of interest in the room.

MANY OF US FACE unsightly heating and ventilation units. The introduction of a low folding screen visually camouflages these obstacles while not interfering with their functions.

SLIPCOVERS   The simplest and least expensive solution to freshening up your rooms and unifying their disparate looks is to slipcover your furniture. A crisp beige linen slipcover over that rolled-arm sofa makes the French side chairs, newly dressed in pale raspberry seersucker, look pretty sensational. Take a few extra yards of that seersucker and whip up two oversize pillows to plump on the sofa, and you're on your way to decorating nirvana. But please don't believe that slipcovers must be loose-fitting. In fact, I much prefer and encourage the opposite. Tailor those babies like a fine suit. Nothing will depress you more than a room full of loose, drooping, baggy slipcovers. It has the allure of a pajama party in a nursing home. Crisp details, like welting or perhaps a smart little contrasting trim at the base of the skirt—and, of course, the best quality nylon zipper so they can be washed and pressed—make all the difference. A word of great caution: If you intend to wash your slipcovers, be certain that the fabric has been prewashed and preshrunk.

UPHOLSTERY   If your furniture is just plain uncomfortable, a simple slipcover won't change that and you may have to consider reupholstering. It can be cheaper than buying new furniture, and it makes sense if you like the basic lines of your piece. On the other hand, the economics of reupholstery can be terrifying. What to do? Here's the quick fix: if you like the style and want to improve the quality, simply replace the foam-filled seat and back cushions with feather or down. The difference will be immediate. And don't worry about matching the fabric. In fact, splurge and get four or five yards of a better-quality fabric that complements the existing cloth on the body of the sofa or chair. Remember, when you're seated, you come in contact not with the body or frame but with the seat and back cushions. That's where luxury matters, so what better place to spend a few extra dollars?

There's really no stopping you now. You've created a beautiful coffered ceiling, established a columned entry, refined those formerly stingy windows and revved up that wild mix of furniture you'd amassed with a few choice slipcovers and new down cushions. These classic examples of transforming plain bad into simple great can direct and inspire us to forge ahead with new self-confidence and creative can-do authority.

HOW TO MAKE THE PERFECT BED

Invariably, the bed is the largest upholstered piece of furniture in the room. Why just let it sit there when it can define all the decorative goals in one package?

Never dress a bed with one brand, style, or color of bedding. This is much too simple, and it robs you of a perfect creative opportunity. Why not buy pillowcases from one vendor, a top sheet from another, and a bottom sheet from someone else? Add that antique quilt your mother gave you, and perhaps borrow a few pillows from your library. Combining these in an artful way and displaying them with originality is an instant room-maker.

9 | DETAILS, DETAILS, DETAILS

Well, you made it! You know how to create a furniture plan. You've figured out how to turn obstacles into surprising advantages. You now understand the inherent joys of manipulating scale and materials. You understand that if you like bright colors, you can have a strong color sensibility and use them with careful abandon. If you like soft colors, you can make rooms whisper. It wasn't as complex as you thought it would be, was it?

With the big picture defined, let us consider what makes a house truly intimate. Intimacy, often, is in the details. At this point you should be asking yourself: How do I get more impact? More design? More power? More satisfaction out of what I'm doing? This is a paradoxical moment in the decorating process. You've finished but, in fact, you're just beginning. This is the stage where we now focus on using decoration and design to create points of emphasis to enhance the foundations we've constructed.

GROUPING OBJECTS BY FORM and color is an ideal way to understand the impact of details. These vases are better displayed together than placed in solitary confinement.

DECORATIVE DETAILS can be well thought out but placed to appear casual. The key is to present them in an approachable format. This entry table has the all hallmarks of effortless placement.

You're finished but, in fact, you're just beginning.

Once again, we're going to tap into our senses. Now it's time to create a visually satisfying juxtaposition of objects, colors, and patterns that establish a design dialogue. For everything that is dark, you want something light. The idea is to establish a relationship from material to material that introduces a push-pull dynamic between opposing complementary finishes, textures, and colors.

Often, people fall in love with a suite of furniture for a dining room or bedroom, but when they get it home they find it bores them into a coma. Why? Because it lacks diversity. That's what details will do—give you diversity, which in turn will establish personality. For example, if you have a series of painted chairs for the dining room, consider pairing them with

Beautiful objects want to be together.

a polished wood table. That kind of contrasting detail between the finishes will activate the two pieces and enable them to enhance each other. For everything that's matte, you want something that's gloss. If you have a wonderful nubby wool sofa, throw a silk or satin pillow on it, so one material is soft and luxurious, and the other has great texture and body.

DON'T FORGET TO ENJOY yourself when exploring the art of placement. This miniature of the Statue of Liberty brings wit to the equation.

Opposites that come together yield a more significant end result. The key is to put elements together so that they give back more than their components. It's what I call the 1 + 1 = 3 Design Theory. By themselves, objects exist in a state of completion. But when combined with something of an opposite shape or finish, the sum is bigger than its parts. The best place to understand how juxtaposition creates style is through the placement of objects. First of all, don't distribute small decorations around the house so that every table has only one or two objects. Instead, start by massing the pieces together to see how their various textures, colors, and shapes establish a dialogue and how they respond in a sensuous way to each other. Wouldn't it be great to see three, five, or seven objects on one table that have an attractive relationship of color and form? Then consider leaving the space next to them empty. This is called negative space, and it can be just as beautiful as filled space.

PICTURE HANGING 101

When it's time to hang artwork, don't do it by remote control. By now you know what I mean—one picture anchored over a chest of drawers or above a sofa and then positioned at a certain level because a friend or relative insisted that pictures have to be a particular height, or you'll be thrown out of the community. Don't even think about picking up a hammer and

PICTURE HANGING is one of the strongest ways to introduce decorative details. I encourage you to be creative in the process. Don't be limited to the standard grid.

THE KEYS TO DIVERSITY

THROUGHOUT THE DESIGN PROCESS, CONTINUALLY INCORPORATE ELEMENTS THAT WILL ENHANCE THE INHERENT QUALITIES OF THE OBJECTS YOU'VE PREVIOUSLY SELECTED. HERE ARE A FEW OF MY FOOLPROOF COMBINATIONS.

- A polished wood dining room table demands painted chairs.
- Place matte objects on a glossy table.
- A nubby wool sofa calls for a satin pillow or two.
- With dark-painted walls, finish the floor in white. With light walls, stain the floors a darker finish.
- To highlight your largest, most important picture, surround it with smaller pictures.

- Group decorative objects by form and color. Mass them rather than distribute them randomly around the house.
- No room is an island. Create rooms that respond to one another rather than isolating them in their own decorative world.
- Just because an object or piece of furniture is beautiful unto itself doesn't validate it as an addition to your decorative program unless it increases the beauty of the objects that surround it.

nail until you review your artwork. Collect all the pictures that you have and lean them up against the wall in a single room. Begin to group those pictures by their relationships of color, size, or subject. When you have created the groupings, move them from room to room to find out which group significantly enhances the beauty and personality of a particular room. When you've finished, you can start hanging.

A great trick for installing groups of artwork is to establish a set amount of space between them. For example, if you want to put five pictures together, consider spacing them three inches apart—and don't deviate from that measurement. That doesn't mean you have to hang them in a row. Instead, hang your second picture three inches above the first and slightly off center, but make the space between them three inches. Then hang the next one

Intimacy is in the details.

three inches to the left of the second picture. Begin to move the pictures up and down, left and right, using intervals of three inches. You're going to have some spaces that are bigger than others, but there will always be at least one point where one frame relates to the other by the same three-inch spacing.

THESE PICTURES are spaced at equal intervals lending a sense of order to the off-center arrangement.

WHY DISTANCE YOURSELF from art? With a picture shelf, you can rearrange your personal collections at whim for a more personal feel. Mix your family photos with paintings, drawings, and sentimental objects.

Before you begin, you may want to do a trial run. Take some brown craft paper, roll it out on the floor, and cut it to the exact size of the available wall space that you have. Lay your grouping on the paper, use a pencil to outline each of the frames, and also mark which image it is. Now take your paper templates and tape them to the wall. You can get the exact nail location for each picture before you start hammering away.

LIGHTING THE WAY Now that we have the furniture in place, the flow of rooms resolved and the pictures hung, we need to highlight those accomplishments with the correct lighting for both atmosphere and function. For all your efforts, nothing will sabotage your hard work faster than a lighting program that hasn't been well planned. Here are the three types that impact a given space the most.

AMBIENT LIGHTING Ambient lighting refers to overall, surrounding light. Before adding 200-watt bulbs to preexisting bare-bulb porcelain fixtures, consider a series of wall-mounted sconces, which will produce more seductively dispersed, easily controlled light than most hanging fixtures and are an excellent alternative to table and floor lamps, which steal surface space and square footage. Don't panic. Wall-mounted lighting is easier to install than you think. Assuming, as is often the case, that any overhead fixture is switched to the wall, you're more than halfway home. Any licensed electrician can take that electrical

location and reroute it to establish sconce locations on the walls. With the addition of a dimmer instead of a switch, you'll instantly attain the desired atmosphere.

Another underused but highly effective lighting trick is metal canister lights (which cost about $15 at most housewares stores). When strategically placed in corners, behind sculptural furniture or plants, these cost-effective wonders cast dramatic, depth-enhancing shadows in controlled areas, defining moments of visual interest. Be certain when purchasing these up lights that they're equipped with a roll switch on the cord. This addition permits you to turn the lights off and on without having to unplug them from the outlet.

OVERHEAD LIGHTING

Overhead lighting continues to get a bum rap. Instead of having it removed, simply correct its unwieldy and unflattering effects. The most immediate solution is to install a dimmer switch. This gives you complete control over the amount of wattage emitted and allows you to create a romantic mood or a utilitarian one.

Additionally, overhead lighting can produce a smoother, more ambient effect by the addition of a carefully thought out shade or cover. While there is an exception to every rule, try to resist the copious supply of overly slick, high-tech scene-stealing light fixtures that currently glut the market. Unless you're moonlighting as a shakedown interrogator, you don't want your guests to spend the evening staring into a naked lightbulb.

IF MANIPULATED CORRECTLY lighting can change the atmosphere of a room. In this entrance hall I used up lights in the corner and behind the carved side chair, which highlights its strong silhouette.

LAMP LIGHTING

Technically, there are two different types of lamp lighting: task lighting and overall lighting. The former assists us in accomplishing specific tasks that require controlled illumination—reading, sewing, and food preparation among them. When purchasing these fixtures, be certain that they will fulfill these goals. Unlike other types of lighting, these are not used simply to light the room.

Overall lighting is the opposite. Classically, when people think of lamp lighting, they see a glazed ceramic form with a translucent shade. This type of lighting is commonly found on a tabletop or as a standing floor lamp. There's tremendous opportunity for decorative flourish, in the base you choose. Unlike task lighting, overall lamp lighting can serve two purposes, either as a reading lamp or as a stylish addition to the atmosphere.

DRAMATIC CONNECTIVITY

We're really into the joys of decorating now, aren't we? So let's achieve some dramatic connectivity. Sounds a little theatrical, I know, but this is critical. A common decorating mistake is isolating the décor of each room. As a result, the rooms are beautiful unto themselves but don't react to the rooms that are next to them. You end up with a French-influenced living room, an Asian-inspired dining room, and a Mediterranean kitchen. Next thing you know, your house has become a Disney theme park, and you are left humming "It's a Small World, After All" and wondering where it all went wrong.

Dramatic connectivity means ensuring that each room is linked to the next by a design element. There has to be a relationship of either color or form. In chapter 6, I introduced the idea of creating some kind of correspondence of wall color from room to room. Now, on a much smaller scale, begin to think about how you might take a few colors from one room and sneak them into the room that adjoins it. You can carry the color through by adding a pillow or two on a sofa or finding other objects that have similar tones, thereby creating an easy transition from space to space.

The same goes for furniture. If you have a dining room with a table and chairs for twelve, do you need to have all twelve chairs at the dining room table all the time? Why not have two of them act as side chairs in the adjoining living room or in your entrance hall? This way, you'll distribute that one shape into different areas of the house. It's a wonderful way to weave one form or one finish throughout the space to unite it.

TRIANGULATION

If dramatic connectivity is now rolling comfortably off your lips, try this one: Color and Pattern Triangulation. It sounds like a technical tongue twister, I know, but it's a critical part of the success of a room. Triangulation means repeating a form, a color, or an object three times in a space. This helps calm down the element and seamlessly introduces the object into your decorative program. For example, if you want a splash of color in a room, don't isolate the color to a throw on the arm of a sofa. You need to repeat the tone in at least two other places in the room. The color can be captured again in a lamp

WHEN ALL THE DETAILS are combined the result is an appealing room that previews elements in the room to follow. This music room seamlessly introduces us to the dining room at the other end (above). DON'T BUY INTO preconceived notions of scale. By placing these fern prints at an unexpected location on the wall, I established an instant dialogue between art and objects (right).

or a pillow on another chair across the room.

When working with objects, think the same way. I've walked into countless living rooms where I'll see a fantastic

HOW TO DRESS THE PERFECT MANTEL:

When all else fails, dress the mantel. If you're fortunate enough to have a fireplace with a modern or antique mantel, it will become the focus of almost any decorative program. Don't waste the opportunity. Here are some pointers.

If you start with the candelabra, you're finished. Avoid the instinct to place a pair of candelabra or tall candlesticks on either outside edge of the mantel. It's predictable and boring, and you're better than that. Instead, think small. A beautiful collection of river stones, a few small votive candles, and perhaps a nosegay of flowers becomes much more satisfying and definitive.

If you must hang a mirror over the mantel, make sure you break up its mass by propping or leaning a few framed watercolors, sketches, or photographs against it to visually break it down. Lastly, never be afraid to change or rotate the objects you display on the mantel. What fun your guests will have as they discover upon every visit the subtle, discreet, and sensitive changes you've created. Don't save this fun just for Christmas.

sculpture resting on a table with no relationship to anything else in the room—odd man out. When you have something special, the tendency is to isolate it in order to show off its inherent beauty. You don't have to have another sculpture to complement it, but you could repeat its color. If it is, for instance, an Asian piece done in a glazed terra-cotta, add something else the same color to the room. If your sculpture is on a stand, perhaps you can put something else on a smaller stand in another area of the room. The aim is to repeat the success of the sculpture's form or color in other materials and locations in the same room.

This tactic highlights the room instead of the object. When experimenting with triangulation, think in threes—a shape, a form, and a color. I'll say it again, and by now you should have this mantra imprinted on your brain: great decorating means that you walk into a room and see its beauty, its sense of welcome, and its completion. You don't remember any single object in it. If your guests enter a room and think, "what a beautiful chair," or "look at that painting," you haven't accomplished what you set

THIS SKETCH ILLUSTRATES that details can often be architectural. The vanity I designed is curved in the front to accommodate easy access to the sink (above). THE SUCCESS OF THIS POWDER ROOM is not dependent on any one object. It's the relationship of circular forms from the sink basin to the ostrich egg on the sill to the porthole window and all the way up to the globe chandelier (right).

out to do. But if they walk into a room and say, "This room is so beautiful; it feels right," then all the details have come together; they're appreciating the overall performance.

THE MATCH GAME If I had to name one word that's been overused in the design world—and the word I hate the most in decorating—it would have to be eclectic. It's too permissive and encourages people to randomly place objects and furniture that don't go together next to each other. When I hear people say, "Oh, I just love the way you mixed everything up," it's like fingernails on the blackboard for me. If that's the case, why don't we just go home and put all of our furniture and objects in a Cuisinart, give it a good chop and whirl, and call it good design?

It's not about the mix; it's about the match. You want to pair objects and furniture that have relationships to each other. As we discussed earlier, it's the curving line next to the straight line that makes us appreciate both. It's the mid-century lacquer chair next to the eighteenth-century Spanish chest that together create a dialogue that activates and informs you about both pieces. There's great energy when you put a carved antique chest of drawers in a modern streamlined house: all of a sudden, the chest pops, and both it and the house look better. Now we're talking. Now we're doing something that translates into personality. And, in the end, that's what we're really trying to do when we're decorating—find ourselves and express who we are.

[ONE OF THE SIMPLEST WAYS to add a personal touch is the thoughtful detail of a throw on a sofa.]

189

10 | DESIGNS
FOR LIVING

I can help you transform your decorating dreams into realistic, attractive, comfortable, modern rooms, but nothing will bring these qualities closer to home than validating them with your personal contributions. Now that you have the rooms you want, how do you live in them? Personally, after I've finished decorating a client's house, the most anticipated final touches are the introduction of a series of intimate details that instantly welcome you to the world of practical beauty.

DESIGNS FOR LIVING
CHAPTER TEN

Traditionally, in eighteenth- and nineteenth-century France and England, architects (who were also known to be decorators) were hired to not only build the structures, but also to furnish them. It was understood that the decorator would provide the basic furnishing foundations for all the rooms, minus the personal details and objects. The enlightened mind's responsibility was to make the house work and the client's responsibility was to give it life. Those life-giving additions were the personal selection of pictures, ceramics, objects, books, lighting, and curtains.

THE DINING ROOM in this apartment clearly reflects the interests of its owner.

BENJAMIN MOORE, MOONLIGHT, 2020-60

SOMETIMES ESTABLISHING a sense of home is as simple as placing potted plants in a room. What it conveys is that the owner cares for her home on a daily basis, not just on special occasions.

Validate rooms
with your personal
contributions.

THIS BEDROOM was converted to a spacious bathroom/dressing room for the ultimate luxury. I set the bathtub by the window to take advantage of the view and added a daybed for serious lounging (above). In this large pool house, intimacy is created by a folding screen that provides privacy for dressing or undressing. The stack of folded towels adds a thoughtful and personal touch (left).

The same can be said today. With the lessons we've learned in the previous chapters, we've come up with a similar foundation, which allows you to plug in your own designs for living.

Never underestimate intimacy as the starting point for a great room.

Here are some suggestions that have never failed to help my clients close the gap between substance and style. The thoughtfulness of these personal touches will long be remembered by family, friends, and—most importantly—you.

In the words of the great Diana Vreeland, why don't you . . .

- Throw caution to the wind and invite your friends over sooner rather than later?

- Break your old habits and have coffee and read the morning paper in the living room?

- Test-drive the guest room by sleeping there one night? Are there enough hangers? Where's the hook for the bathroom? Placing a few bestsellers and magazines in the room won't hurt, either.

- Establish a gallery of cherished family photos assembled in a hallway, using white frames for all?

- Have a picnic in front of the fire? (If you have a fireplace, that is.)

- Light the candles in the dining room and have a family dinner?

- Place an attractive container of sharpened pencils and a stack of notepads next to every phone? Points up, please.

- Put fresh-cut flowers on the bedside table (even if you don't expect guests)?

- Welcome winter with an enormous bowl of clementines in your entry hall?

- Place a stack of bandanas in the powder room to be used as guest towels?

- Turn off the television and tune in the stereo?

- Ask your children what color they want their room to be?

HOW TO MAKE THE PERFECT FLOWER ARRANGEMENT:

Don't be scared. Contrary to our learned insecurities, we're all capable of making the perfect flower arrangement. It starts with scissors. Just because they're sold to you as long-stem roses doesn't mean they have to stay that way. The same goes for tulips, daisies, daffodils, lilies, you name it. Dramatically cutting down the stems on all of the flowers and tightly arranging them in any container (as simple as a juice glass or as plain as a coffee mug) will be an instant triumph.

These suggestions are but a few of the thousands of options we have each day to improve our houses, our lives, and ourselves. There is a wonderful, old-fashioned French saying that translates to, "Given a dollar, spend fifty cents on bread and fifty cents on flowers." It means that once the substance of life has been resolved, beauty must have equal value. The joys of creating house and home are now in your enlightened hands. Simple, thoughtful, charming details, like flowers, scented

Your personality is as individual as your fingerprint.

candles, hand-pressed pillowcases, and strategically placed notepads and pencils promote the ultimate luxury—that of sensitively caring for your well-being, the pleasure of your family, the comfort of your friends, and the satisfaction of seeing everything come seamlessly together.

Welcome Home!

FOR THIS HOUSE the owners change the living room to reflect the seasons. In summer, they roll up the wool area rug and replace it with a small straw carpet to expose the cool hardwood floors. The furniture is slipcovered in white cotton. In winter the room is focused on the fireplace and returned to its rich palette of amber and brown.

One of the qualities I look for in designers for my company is a sound understanding of the basic foundations and vocabulary of great design. Without these tools, more often than not, you're at the mercy of the salesperson or the vendor. With them, you're free to not only be your creative best but also to enjoy the net results of your knowledge and input.

Let's examine five of the make-or-break nitty-gritty details that will elevate your design solutions to the very best of modern living.

Lighting

The great success of properly planned lighting is more than a beautiful shade or a pretty shape. Besides beauty, light must ultimately be practical. Let's examine some of its components.

SWITCHING
There are many types of switches that can be added or subtracted to table or floor lamps. All of them make a great difference in how you use and benefit from your lamps.

THREE-WAY
The three-way bulb is perhaps the greatest invention since the bulb itself. A three-way switch combined with a three-way bulb gives you the flexibility to adjust the light level in any room, depending on need or mood. This is especially appropriate for reading locations, such as a bedside lamp or a table lamp next to a chair in the library. The most effective wattage of a three-way bulb is a combination of thirty/seventy/one-hundred watts. This permits soft lighting when relaxing and bright lighting for reading. Although many combinations of three-way bulbs exist, start here and see if this one suits your needs.

DIMMERS OR REOSTATS
What you know as dimmers the interior design and building trade know as reostats. Don't be confused—they're the same thing.

Nothing changes the atmosphere of a room more rapidly and less expensively than a dimmer and a lightbulb. Many times, your apartment or house will have two switches at the door—one connected to an overhead fixture and another unbeknownst to you, connected to an outlet mysteriously located somewhere in the room. Find that outlet.

This is accomplished simply by putting the switch in the off position, and walking about the room with any lightweight table lamp in the on position. Insert the lamp into both top and bottom of the duplex outlet and return to the switch location. Flipping the switch on will tell you whether that is the link outlet or not. Once located, you've found the mood maker. That switch should immediately be changed to a dimmer. What you're going to gain by connecting one or many lamps to that dimmer is the ability to immediately transform the beauty and seductiveness of the room by having the option of changing the level of light the moment you enter the room.

WATTAGE
I'll keep this short. Don't, don't, don't over-light your life. The amount of times I've walked into a client's apartment where 2,500 watts were burning in every room would surprise you. If your at-home hobby is diamond cutting, this lighting scheme is terrific. Otherwise, it will kill any pleasure you would get from a beautifully decorated house.

I suggest that you start with bulbs twenty-five watts or less than what you think you need. Higher wattage isn't necessarily better.

LAMPS

There are thousands of varieties of lamps, but only four basic categories. Here they are and here's what they do:

TABLETOP LIGHTING

A tabletop lamp is the best way to add light and decoration to any room, providing the opportunity for not only a beautiful shade in linen, paper, or silk, but also a moment of creative expression in the form and material you choose for the base. Whether you converted an old bottle or used a nineteeth-century pitcher, the decorative choice is yours and the impact is substantial.

TASK LIGHTING

This is the workhorse of the lighting world. As the name implies, task lighting helps you accomplish the task at hand, whether it's working at your desk, chopping vegetables in the kitchen, or putting together a ship model at your hobby table. With task lighting, you can begin to explore the world of low wattage, halogen, and tensor lighting. All of these assist you by delivering a better quality of pure, white light. For instance, think how much more sparkle and light your diamond ring had when you looked at it in the jewelers' case versus when you look at it on your hand now.

TENT LIGHTING

Boy, do tent lights do their job! That job is to help you light rooms without looking as if you own a lampshade shop. The goal when planning a lighting program for any room is a balanced combination of lamps with shades and lamps with tents. A tent is an opaque shade, typically made of metal and in the form of a small pup tent. Think of an A-frame house. What a tent lamp does is throw light down onto a book or tabletop without allowing light to escape from the top, as it does from a shaded lamp.

UP LIGHTS

I've saved the best for last. Here's the biggest magic trick I know and a hallmark of my style. Almost all lighting stores sell up lights, sometimes known as can lights. These are cylindrical or rectangular lamps that sit directly on the floor and contain an upward-facing flood light. They can be either switched on and off directly from the cord, or, if you're really observant and have found that wired switch outlet, connected directly to your newly installed reostat. With a little luck and a multiple-socket extension cord, you can connect three or four up lights to a single dimmer. From that one location, you can manipulate the appearance and atmosphere of the entire room. I can't emphasize enough that nothing is more successful than an up light.

Upholstery

It's all in the details. As a professional, I can spot a well-made, well-designed chair from the door. With these tips, you can too.

SHAPE

Like our bodies, there are many different ways to describe our shape or form. The same is true when discussing upholstery. Here are some of the basic names and options you should be looking for when commissioning upholstery or talking to a salesman about your specific needs when shopping for furniture in department stores.

SQUARE BACK

As the name implies, square back signifies the outer back of any sofa or chair with a straight or square edge. Although not the most exciting of shapes, this shape was specifically designed so that furniture could sit squarely up against a wall.

SCROLL BACK

The scroll back is a much softer, rounded form than the square back. Because its curves emphasize its back and sides, use a scroll back when a piece is going to be seen from all directions in a room–for instance, a sofa in the middle of a room close to the fireplace.

SKIRTS

As in fashion, there are many types of skirts, each of which is a product of its times and purpose. Two of the most common are:

ENGLISH EDGE

The English edge was developed in the late nineteenth century and is still popular today. The skirt drops from the edge of the platform of the upholstered furniture (the platform being the area on which the seat cushion rests). The English edge is rolled and is clearly noticeable in the form of a half-round [it looks like a half-circle]. Underneath that half-round, the skirt is attached and drops to the floor.

WATERFALL

The waterfall skirt was developed in the mid-twentieth century to streamline and modernize old-fashioned forms. The equivalent of an upholstery facelift, it is still the most successful way to rejuvenate traditional forms. As the name implies, the waterfall skirt starts at the edge of the platform and cascades in a straight run down to the floor.

DETAILS

Following is the vocabulary everyone needs to know when ordering upholstered furniture from a store or when working directly from an upholstery workroom to create the chair or sofa of your dreams.

WELTING

Welting, or piping, is a small, raised tube of fabric that is commonly used at the seams of a piece of furniture. There are two different types:

SELF-WELT: Consists of the same material as the body of the chair or the cushion. Meaning, if you have blue chair, your self-welting will also be blue.

CONTRAST WELT: Uses a different or contrasting material for the welting. For instance, a blue chair could sport a contrast welt of bright yellow to bring out its form and details.

TAPE

Tape, preferably no larger than ¾-inch and usually cut on the bias or at a forty-five degree angle, is commonly used at the base of a skirt or on the frame of a chair. This is the perfect way to finish the weld-detail upholstery, providing a logical conclusion to the upholstered form, separating it from the carpet or floor below. There are two types:

SELF-TAPE: As with self-welt, self-tape adds the most discreet and subtle of details by using the same fabric as the body of the chair, turned on the bias, and reapplied to the furniture.

CONTRAST TAPE: As with contrast welt, contrast tape uses a different or contrasting fabric to add a noticeable finishing detail. For instance, a skirted beige chair can happily sport a ¾-inch red contrast tape.

Paint

There are two distinct categories of paint.

ALKYD OR OIL-BASED

The industry name for what used to be known as oil-based paint is alkyd. Alkyd is an invaluable material for painting any or all woodwork, such as doors, door frames, windows, and baseboards. It is a stronger and more durable material than Latex and is ideal for enhancing luster and sheen, which brings out the natural details in any millwork. It can only be removed with paint thinner or turpentine.

LATEX

What we used to know as water-based paint is actually Latex. Latex is the primary paint used on walls and ceilings. It is best used as a flat finish, since these surfaces are more color than finish-driven. Latex paints can be removed with soap and water.

Carpets

There are two basic categories:

WALL-TO-WALL

Wall-to-wall is today's most commonly used carpet, primarily because new construction seldom allows the luxury of hardwood floors and instead have wooden subfloors of plywood or, in apartments, poured concrete. Wall-to-wall is the perfect way to disguise these conditions. As the name implies, the carpet is installed from one wall to the other without exposing any of the floor beneath it. This method can be installed with tackless, which is a wooden strip with exposed nails or tacks at the outside edges of the room. The carpet is installed directly to these tacks, which hold it in place. An increasingly more common installation is called glue-down. This does not involve the use of tackless at all, but, in fact, means the carpet is glued directly to the floor with a Latex adhesive. Wall-to-wall is the quickest, cheapest method to carpet a large area.

AREA RUGS

If you're fortunate enough to have hardwood floors or attractive ceramic tiles, such as terra-cotta, use new or antique area rugs to leave some of that floor exposed. A good rule of thumb is to leave at least two feet of floor exposed all around the room. So if your room is ten feet by ten feet, an area rug eight feet by eight feet would be ideal.

Window Treatments

There are endless ways to dress a window. Let's examine the top three:

CURTAINS

Over the last twenty years, curtains—deemed old-fashioned and fussy—have suffered a decline in popularity. Forget those preconceived ideas and recall the images you've seen in this book. Think how modern and light curtains can be. And curtains aren't just for decoration—they also serve a purpose.

CURTAIN TYPES

There are two types of curtains, lined and unlined. The difference in feel and function is like the difference between your winter coat and linen blazer.

LINED: In the past, curtains were almost always lined to block out furniture-fading sunlight, as well as to insulate against the heat and the cold. There are still uses for lined curtains. If you live in an area that's cold most of the year, lined curtains provide an additional buffer between your rooms and the outside world. If you like to sleep in, lined curtains provide terrific room-darkening qualities.

UNLINED: If you have new windows with built-in UVA screens that block the damaging effects of sunlight, you are free to use unlined curtains. These curtains can actually enhance the sense of light in a room for the simple reason that when we see the sunlight through the curtain's material, we become more conscious of it. For this reason, unlined curtains are especially successful in rooms with limited light.

CURTAIN TERMINOLOGY

When ordering curtains by phone or commissioning them through a work room, a knowledge of certain words will guarantee the success of your order.

EDGES: All four edges of a curtain have different names and can, in fact, be treated differently:

HEADING: The top edge of the curtain where, more often than not, you will find a pleat. There are numerous types of pleating and ways to finish the heading which should be discussed with the manufacturer.

LEADING: The leading edge is the inside edge of the curtain, meaning the side farthest from the frame. This is often a great place for an additional detail, such as a contrast tape.

OUTSIDE: As the name suggests, the outside edge is the edge closest to the frame. It is the opposite of the leading edge.

BOTTOM: The bottom edge touches the window sill or rests on the floor. A simple and successful detail for the bottom edge is its break. As the cuff of your pants breaks on your shoe, a curtain should have an extra inch of fabric at the bottom that rests on the floor, commonly known as a puddle.

SHADES

One of the more practical ways to dress windows is with shades, which can be used with or without curtains.

SHADE TYPES

ROMAN: A Roman shade can be lined or unlined and is pleated horizontally—much the same way an accordion is pleated. Roman shades are tailored, crisp, and contemporary.

BALLOON: As the name suggests, a balloon shade is full and voluminous. Balloon shades are soft, romantic, and old-fashioned.

SOLAR: The most modern option is a solar shade. For years, solar shades have been used successfully in offices and museums. They are identical to old-fashioned roller shades except that they have been updated to prevent solar heat and UVA infiltration but still permit us to see through an outside the window, even in the down position.

SHUTTERS

Shutters are increasingly popular because of their versatility and affordability. Shutters originated in the tropics, but are now available and used in all climates. Some specifics when ordering shutters should be known.

SHUTTER TYPES

OPERABLE OR FIXED: An operable shutter is one that allows you to adjust the angle of the louvers or slats without opening or closing the shutter itself.

FIXED: A fixed shutter means the louvers or slats are fixed or set in one position and cannot be moved. The only way to let light in or block it out is to open and close the shutters themselves.

TWO OVER TWO / FOUR OVER FOUR / SIX OVER SIX: This is not new math. These are the specifications that you will be asked to provide when ordering shutters. It's the simple designation of how many shutters you'd like on the bottom and top of your window, split horizontally when hung. For instance, four over four means that you have four pair of shutters on one window, two pair on the bottom and two pair on the top, making a total of eight, therein four over four.

ACKNOWLEDGEMENTS

This first book would have been impossible without the trust and enthusiasm of all my clients. They came to me for knowledge and direction, but in trade, returned it with their own insights and goals for each project. I've often remarked that I'm only as good as my last project. In fact, each and every client has made a contribution to the success of that next project, the one that's better than the last.

Some client relationships have developed into friendships that continue to deepen as their projects evolve. For that, I am truly grateful.

In a business that emphasizes the "acquisitive," I have been fortunate to know those people whose priorities focused on the "inquisitive." Without the ability to understand ourselves and the world we create around us, beauty is not attainable.

My gratitude to the many who have opened their doors and shared their souls. I am certain that together we have created joy.

PHOTOGRAPHERS' APPENDIX

ANTOINE BOOTZ has enjoyed a successful career with various high profile editorial and commercial clients.

FRANCOIS DISHCHINGER, New Yorker, photographer

OBERTO GILI, photographer

KARI HAAVISTO is a prize-winning photographer whose work has appeared in *House Beautiful*, *Architectural Digest*, and *Town and Country*.

FRANCOIS HALARD collaborates regularly with *Vogue US*, *Vanity Fair*, *GQ*, and *House & Garden*.

THIBAULT JEANSON counts almost every major interiors publication as a client, including *Vogue*, *Elle Décor*, *Martha Stewart Living*, *House & Garden*, *House Beautiful*, and *World of Interiors*.

SCOTT FRANCES is a contributing photographer to *Architectural Digest* and has also been the exclusive photographer documenting the work of architect Richard Meier for the past decade.

LIZZIE HIMMEL works for numerous editorial publications, including *The New York Times Sunday Magazine*, *Harper's Bazaar*, *Elle Décor*, *Rolling Stone*, and most Condé Nast publications.

PETER MARGONELLI has brought his sensibility to such publications as *House Beautiful*, *Real Simple*, and *House & Garden* and has two books in print on the use of color in interiors and bath style for *Waterworks*.

DEAN PENNA, president of Penna Inc., a painting company that's been in business for fourteen years, specializes in high-end residential work.

WILLIAM WALDRON is a freelance photographer whose clients include *Elle Décor*, *Real Simple*, *Vogue*, *Southern Accents*, Trish McEvoy, Ltd., and W Hotels.

INDEX

ABOUT THE AUTHOR

From the cobblestones and shingles of Nantucket (where Bilhuber has his own summer retreat) to the posh streets of New York's Upper East Side, Jeffrey Bilhuber has been making his mark in the interior design field for nearly 20 years. His unique interpretation of "American Classicism," which combines classic forms with a modernist context, has continued to attract a wide and diverse client base. His work has been featured in *Architectural Digest*, *House Beautiful*, *House & Garden*, *Elle Décor*, *W* magazine, the *New York Times*, and *Vogue*, as well as on CNN, "Late Night with Conan O'Brien," ABC's "The View," and HGTV's "Public Places, Private Spaces."

Ocean A

New York City Hand Woven S
Farmstands
Celadon Ice Blue Fre
Children's Laughter Honesty Garli
Sandy Beaches • Suede Good Healt
Roaring Fires
All That Jazz People Who Love
Friends
Sweet Peas
Walking barefoot in the grass Meatloaf Cand
Discretion Garden
Homemade Chili Without Beans Going to the Movies in th
The Perfect Mar